THE COMPLETE IDIOT'S GUIDE® TO

Stretching Your Dollar

by Shannon M. Medisky

ALPHA

A member of Penguin Group (USA) Inc.

ALPHA BOOKS

Published by the Penguin Group

Penguin Group (USA) Inc., 375 Hudson Street, New York, New York 10014, USA

Penguin Group (Canada), 90 Eglinton Avenue East, Suite 700, Toronto, Ontario M4P 2Y3, Canada (a division of Pearson Penguin Canada Inc.)

Penguin Books Ltd., 80 Strand, London WC2R 0RL, England

Penguin Ireland, 25 St. Stephen's Green, Dublin 2, Ireland (a division of Penguin Books Ltd.)

Penguin Group (Australia), 250 Camberwell Road, Camberwell, Victoria 3124, Australia (a division of Pearson Australia Group Pty. Ltd.)

Penguin Books India Pvt. Ltd., 11 Community Centre, Panchsheel Park, New Delhi—110 017, India

Penguin Group (NZ), 67 Apollo Drive, Rosedale, North Shore, Auckland 1311, New Zealand (a division of Pearson New Zealand Ltd.)

Penguin Books (South Africa) (Pty.) Ltd., 24 Sturdee Avenue, Rosebank, Johannesburg 2196, South Africa

Penguin Books Ltd., Registered Offices: 80 Strand, London WC2R 0RL, England

Copyright © 2009 by Shannon M. Medisky

International Standard Book Number: 978-1-59257-928-0
Library of Congress Catalog Card Number: 2009923297

11   10   09   8   7   6   5   4   3   2   1

Interpretation of the printing code: The rightmost number of the first series of numbers is the year of the book's printing; the rightmost number of the second series of numbers is the number of the book's printing. For example, a printing code of 09-1 shows that the first printing occurred in 2009.

Printed in the United States of America

Note: This publication contains the opinions and ideas of its author. It is intended to provide helpful and informative material on the subject matter covered. It is sold with the understanding that the author and publisher are not engaged in rendering professional services in the book. If the reader requires personal assistance or advice, a competent professional should be consulted.

The author and publisher specifically disclaim any responsibility for any liability, loss, or risk, personal or otherwise, which is incurred as a consequence, directly or indirectly, of the use and application of any of the contents of this book.

Most Alpha books are available at special quantity discounts for bulk purchases for sales promotions, premiums, fund-raising, or educational use. Special books, or book excerpts, can also be created to fit specific needs.

For details, write: Special Markets, Alpha Books, 375 Hudson Street, New York, NY 10014.

Publisher: *Marie Butler-Knight*

Editorial Director: *Mike Sanders*

Senior Managing Editor: *Billy Fields*

Executive Editor: *Randy Ladenheim-Gil*

Senior Development Editor: *Christy Wagner*

Senior Production Editor: *Megan Douglass*

Copy Editor: *Jan Zoya*

Cover Designer: *Becky Harmon*

Book Designer: *Trina Wurst*

Indexer: *Tonya Heard*

Layout: *Ayanna Lacey*

Proofreader: *Mary Hunt*

Contents at a Glance

Contents

Introduction

Everything costs more these days, and you seem to be spending more on the same items you've been buying for years—and you're *not* getting more for your money. How can you continue to buy what you need without continually increasing your spending? The answer: you learn how to stretch your dollar.

When I quit my full-time job to stay at home and care for our children, I knew I was also taking on a new job—full-time economist—and I soon came to realize that when it comes to money and making ends meet, necessity is indeed the mother of invention. There *are* ways to make those proverbial ends meet, or at least get a little closer, and that doesn't have to mean drastically changing your lifestyle.

After wasting shameful amounts of money on magazines with headlines touting ways to save, I finally realized there are no real get-something-for-nothing, get-rich-quick tricks. Article after article told me what I already knew: make a budget and know how much money was going where. Well, duh, but where was the information to show me *how* to stretch the money I had? Out of necessity, I created new tactics for applying these commonsense techniques to stretch my dollar further. Rather than constantly worrying about how to bring in more money, I shifted my efforts toward how to get more for the money I had.

I want to emphasize the most important thing I've learned along the way: the more effort you apply to stretching your dollar, the more success you'll see. You don't have to apply all these tactics all the time to benefit from them, but the more you do, the more rewarded your bottom line will be.

In these difficult economic times, it can sometimes feel as if your finances are spinning out of control as the value of the dollar declines and prices go up. Use this book as your guide to maneuvering your spending in a tactical way. Outsmart the advertisers, demand more from what you purchase, and empower yourself to spend less while getting more. I know you can do it!

How to Use This Book

The first four chapters of this book cover the general how, when, where, and what to do to stretch and save your dollar. The information in these chapters is designed to help empower you to get more for your dollar in any situation and inspire you to find even more ways to whittle down your costs.

The remaining chapters cover specific ways to apply these concepts. While some of the ideas covered may seem overtly obvious, they are included because they obviously do work, and they're later expanded upon in new ways.

Use this book to learn *all* the possible ways to stretch your dollar and how you can train yourself to discover new money-saving tactics to apply to your own situation.

Little Extras

Throughout the book you'll also find sidebars to aid you in learning how to stretch your dollar. Here's what to look for:

Penny Pitfall

These boxes alert you to warnings to heed and ways to look out for your dollar.

def•i•ni•tion

These boxes define terms every serious dollar stretcher needs to know.

Dollar $tretcher

Look to these boxes for quick and easy tips and tricks to make your dollar really s-t-r-e-t-c-h.

Super Saver

Here you'll find bits of information you may not have known that help you further stretch and save your bucks.

Acknowledgments

I'd like to thank my best friend and partner in life, Jason. I will never take the life we've built together for granted. You have my gratitude and love forever. Thanks also to our two sons, Nate and Mark, who give me the incentive to be the best steward of our resources I can be. Thank you to my Creator for giving me the ability to seek creative solutions and the gift of finding contentment with what I already have.

Trademarks

All terms mentioned in this book that are known to be or are suspected of being trademarks or service marks have been appropriately capitalized. Alpha Books and Penguin Group (USA) Inc. cannot attest to the accuracy of this information. Use of a term in this book should not be regarded as affecting the validity of any trademark or service mark.

How to Save Money

In This Chapter

- What and who you need to know to save
- DIY clearance items
- When to buy quality
- Cash, check, or credit?
- Great ways to get and use coupons

If you're like most people, at one time or another (probably more recently than not) you've stood at the cash register waiting with slight trepidation for the total to ring up, or you've looked down at your outgoing bills with a flutter of fear in your heart. Rest assured, you're not alone.

We all want to maintain our current lifestyle while reducing the amount of money we spend to have it, right? Does that seem like wishful thinking to you? Well, it's not! Stop wishing and make it happen. The tips and techniques in this book can help you keep your shopping cart just as full while you save money. That's what stretching your dollar is all about: more for less.

Knowledge Is Your Key to Savings

Ignorance may be bliss in some situations, but it's certainly not when it comes to saving money. Simply not knowing any better leaves you victim to higher prices, shoddy quality, and fewer options. Lack of knowledge isn't an excuse, but it may very well be the reason many people don't get the most from their money.

Educating yourself doesn't have to be drag, though. In fact, it can be fun because getting more for less can be a great challenge. Turn it into a game to see how much more you can get while keeping your spending at the same level it is now (or even dropping it!). Some things will be easy, while others will be more challenging. For instance, for small purchases, all you might have to do to stretch your dollar is simply look at all the options on the store shelf before putting something in your cart. On the other hand, major purchases will likely require more effort because more of your money is at stake.

The good news is that the more effort you put in to acquire all this spending knowledge, the more you'll be rewarded when you shell out less money at the cash register and keep more green in your wallet.

What You Need to Know

Let's start with the *what* of stretching your dollars. If you've ever read anything on how to save money, you've likely heard it said time and time again: make a list and know what you're going to get before you go shopping. This is true, but there's a lot more worth figuring out before you plunk down your money.

Decide in advance exactly what you need to get out of your purchase so you'll know how much money to invest in it. Advertisers pay big bucks to entice you to purchase their products. Knowing exactly what you want helps you withstand the siren song of more than you need, not to mention the advertising ploys. Sometimes good enough really is; don't allow yourself to get talked into—and pay for—more.

Whether you're looking for something on the cheap or looking to invest in a long-term purchase, you can't identify a great price without first knowing the item's various price extremes. Do some research—in stores, online, or both—to become knowledgeable in price ranges and what exactly you can expect to get for each price point. You may very well know you want a bare-bones coffeemaker. But unless you know what a fair price for that appliance is, you leave yourself vulnerable to paying an espresso-machine price. (For easy online price comparisons, see Resources.)

A great resource for both price and quality comparison just so happens to be a free one, *Consumer Reports*. Their tagline, "expert, independent, nonprofit," says it all. A quick look www.consumerreports.org can immediately help you determine what a fair price is for nearly anything. And because they're nonprofit, you can rest assured that the information you're getting is as unbiased as it can get.

Who You Need to Know

So you know what you're buying, but what about *who* you're buying it from or *who* can help you save? I'm sure you've heard that networking can do great things for your career; it can also do amazing things for your wallet. Sometimes it's just as much about who you know as what you know. Tell me who your friends are, and I'll tell you how you can save money—it's the "stretching your dollar network," as I like to call it.

The easiest way to start your network is to get your friends onboard. You can often get a great price by asking your friends to shop for you. Senior citizens can take advantage of senior discount days at a variety of different locations, including discount retail stores and thrift shops. Store employees often get store discounts where they work.

Teachers can get lower prices nearly everywhere. By simply showing a school ID badge, pay stub, or other proof of affiliation, educators can snag discounts at bookstores, office supply stores, and even software manufacturers. Some teacher discounts are reserved for classroom purchases only, but more and more retailers are offering the discount as a way to thank the educators in the community and are allowing them to take advantage of the savings on all purchases—professional and personal.

> **Dollar $tretcher**
>
> Educator discounts aren't reserved for in-classroom teachers. Many retailers offer the same discount privileges to librarians and homeschoolers. Be sure to ask if your affiliation qualifies you for such savings.

If you're able to get such friends to make a discounted purchase on your behalf, be sure to not wear out your welcome to similar savings in the future. Show your gratitude for their assistance in helping you save, and reimburse them promptly. And maybe offer them some similar help if you have shopping perks your friends don't have.

Creative Ways to Spend and Still Save

Sure, the easiest way to save money is to not spend it. But a person's still gotta live, right? So the next best thing is to be sure you spend the least amount possible. No one's in the business of giving money away, so don't give away yours unnecessarily either. Get creative about finagling a cheaper price, and get in the business of keeping your wallet full.

The easiest and most effective way to get creative about spending is to find new ways to use tried-but-true techniques. People still use coupons because they do help save money. Just don't limit yourself to traditional sources. Clearance and discount bins offer great savings, but don't wait for items to end up there before you seek the cheaper price: take control yourself! Loyalty card programs can reward you for shopping at a particular store, but increase the card's savings potential by using it in different ways. Let's take a closer look at discounts and loyalty cards.

Devise Your Own Discounts

Take the initiative, and ask for discounts that aren't even offered. Be open to outright asking for discounts for less-than-perfect products or packaging. If you're not worried about getting the original packaging with your purchase, ask if floor models are available for purchase at a discount. And if you purchase an appliance without a manual or the original packaging, have no fear. Most manufacturers provide full, printable manuals for their appliances online.

Another easy way to snag a lower price is to point out product or packaging flaws. If you see a tear in a package, a small dent in an appliance, a missing button, or any other cosmetic imperfection, don't wait for a markdown that you might miss. Bring it to the manager's attention now; ask for a discount and you may very well receive it. The very worst that can happen is he'll say no and you'll be left paying no more than you would've before. Give it a try, and you might be surprised at how much you save.

From booking travel arrangements to unadvertised specials at retail locations to special long-distance phone rates, don't miss an opportunity to ask if any discounts or special offers are available. Many special pricing opportunities aren't advertised and are only offered to those who ask. Resolve to be one of the lucky few. Repeat after me: *I will take the initiative!*

Let Loyalty Pay You Back

Many stores and even restaurants offer loyalty programs to help encourage repeat business. If you see this as nothing more than a marketing ploy, you're absolutely right. With every wave of your card, the store can track your spending and monitor your purchase habits. If you're willing to give up a little of your anonymity, you can rack up significant benefits, including savings. Depending on the specific loyalty program, you might get special pricing, free items, or even rebate checks. The benefits don't have to stop there, though.

Many supermarkets either partner with local gas stations or have their own and offer per-gallon discounts to loyalty card users, for example. (More information on this loyalty card savings technique can be found in Chapter 6.)

If your store prints out coupons at the cash register, use this purchase tracking system to your advantage. Purposefully alternate the different brands you purchase. Each time you shop, you'll increase your chances of "earning" a coupon for a competitor's brand of the same product.

Another way to get more coupon variety and rack up a higher rebate is to hand out all those extra cards you received when you initially signed up. If friends or family decide not to sign up for their own account, ask if they would be

 Super Saver _____

Need more loyalty cards than you were given when you signed up? Pick up a new set and call the customer information line. Ask that the new cards be linked to your existing account. You'll have more cards available to help you accrue points and rebates faster.

willing to carry and scan your card for their purchases. They'll receive any available savings on the spot, and you'll accrue their rebate points. Last year, a friend of mine got a free turkey for Thanksgiving just for using her loyalty card at her supermarket.

Buyer Beware

Not overpaying is key, but being sure you buy lasting value is even more important. Cheaper is not always better; quantity and quality are both important. Know when paying a little extra can afford you better value.

Look for products by manufacturers that will stand behind their products. Keep in mind, too, that *guarantees* are always a better value than *warranties*. Regardless, don't pay for your own mistake when you can learn from somebody else's. Talk to friends and family to find out if they have any experience with a brand or product. Or check out Internet sites that provide a platform to openly review products for the benefit of other consumers (see Resources). It never hurts to ask at the customer service desk if they get many returns of the particular product, either.

def•i•ni•tion

A **warranty** protects a manufacturer by defining limitations for what they'll do in the event something goes wrong with a product. A **guarantee** protects consumers by promising their satisfaction with a product or service.

The more major the purchase, the more important it can be to buy from a reputable retailer. Double your buyer protection by not only purchasing from a manufacturer willing to stand behind the product, but also from a retailer willing to stand behind your purchase. A store that offers a longer return or exchange period can help protect you further should that purchase go kaput too soon.

Ongoing Operational Costs

If you're in the market for a product that will have ongoing costs, don't forget to consider those also prior to making a purchase. A cheaper appliance that has costly accessories, refills, or filters is no deal at all.

Many manufacturers will purposefully price their items low to rope consumers into paying more for additional costs over the life of the product. Paying a bit more upfront for an item that has lower ongoing costs can be the best way to get more for less.

For example, when you're in the market for a home printer, ask store employees which printer features cartridges that are easily refillable. Even if you opt out of refilling cartridges, there's still great savings to be had. Search eBay for your printer's replacement cartridges. You're sure to find either discounted manufacturer or generic cartridges brand new for less than you'd pay in the store.

The following list shows a few examples of the kinds of products that require ongoing operational expenses:

Product	Needed Supplies
Home printer	Ink cartridges, paper
Photo printer	Toner/ink, photo paper
Fax machine	Toner or cartridges, paper
Water filtration	Filters
Vacuum (upright and handheld)	Filters, bags
Digital camera	Memory cards, batteries
Car	License plates, insurance

The information is easy to attain and the savings can be great, so jot down the name and model number to scope out the ongoing operational costs either in the store or online. Do be careful, though, as store brands as well as generic competitor brands can all vary greatly in price as well as quality. You can even ask a repair service which model historically breaks down the least.

It can pay to check for online reviews of accessories as well. Items such as generic video game accessories may not pose any harm to the actual system itself, but low-quality ink may do damage to a printer. Do some research before you plunk down your money.

More to Love?

Our high-tech society seems obsessed with appliances that multi-task as much as we do. These appliances can be great budget stretchers, but they can also create more problems when something goes awry. You may be able to live without your scanner for a few days if your 3-in-1 printer, scanner, fax machine breaks, but it may be more difficult to cope without TV if your combined TV/DVD player stops working.

Consider in advance how reliant you are on specific appliance tasks, and purchase multifunction appliances accordingly. Remember, it's the manufacturer's job to try to con you into thinking you need more. Do you really need a toaster oven with a separate toasting function on top for bread and bagels? On the other hand, a video game console that doubles as a DVD player may be expensive initially but can be a worthwhile investment as an entertainment powerhouse.

How to Pay to Lower Your Costs

We're increasingly becoming a cashless society. My 3-year-old son knows how to use an ATM (yes, I let him push the buttons) but is still having difficulty grasping that nickels are worth more than pennies. The old saying of "money is money" is quickly becoming *not* the case.

The method of payment you choose to use can often have a profound effect on the price you end up paying after all's said and done. Know when to use the various methods to pay and you'll not only lower your bottom line, but ensure you get more for your dollar, too.

Credit Cards

Credit cards aren't inherently evil; they are a financial tool like any other form of payment. Be wise in how you use them, and they can work to your advantage. If you're making a major purchase and a sales associate offers you a discount if you sign up for the store's credit card, consider it. Charge the total purchase to the new credit card to receive the lower price and then pay in full as soon as you receive the bill. (Feel free to close the account quickly as well.)

Many credit cards also offer reward programs as a way to attract and keep business. Use this to your advantage to earn rebate checks or free items by using your credit card to purchase everyday items. Just be mindful to pay the balance due in full immediately, or you may actually end up owing more in the form of interest. One of my friends uses the gift cards she earns from spending on her American Express card during the year (and paying her bill off every month) as holiday gifts for all her nieces and nephews.

Major credit card issuers such as American Express, Visa, and Master-Card also offer complimentary extended warranties for qualified purchases. All you have to do is pay for the entire item using your credit card and then register the product with your credit card company. It will afford you extra protection for your purchase and cost you absolutely nothing.

 Super Saver _____

If you use your credit card often, link your credit card account to your bank account either through the creditor or the bank directly so you can transfer money immediately to pay off purchases even before you receive the bill. This means no postage paid and often no interest accrued. Even if you're unable to pay the balance in full, you'll be better equipped to keep the balance from growing.

Debit, Check, and ATM Cards

Check and debit cards offer the convenience of a credit card with the peace of mind that comes without accruing debt. They're not only convenient, but can save and even earn you money, too.

Using a debit card reduces the number of trips you have to make to an ATM to get cash, saving you money on ATM fees. If you have to pay for check printing, using your card can save you money by minimizing the number of checks you write. And with some debit cards, you can earn rebates offered by some banks, credit unions, and even retailers such as IKEA. Even PayPal.com offers a debit card (linked to your free PayPal account) that pays 1.5 percent cash back on all debit purchases.

Don't get complacent about the convenience, though. Remember to save receipts to reconcile with your check register later, or—better yet—subtract the purchase amount on the spot. It can be easy to forget a purchase here and there, especially the small ones. They add up quickly, though, and a molehill of forgotten debit purchases can add up to a mountain of expensive overdraft fees.

Penny Pitfall

Remember, your debit card enables businesses to deduct funds from your checking account immediately. To avoid any possible overdraft fees, ask your bank to link your checking account to your savings account for overdraft protection. If this isn't available, consider opening a line of credit through the bank for just this purpose.

Cold, Hard Cash

Even in this day and age of electronic money transfers and automated banking, there's still the practice of "cash only." There are costs involved in processing credit and debit card purchases. Many businesses are rewarding the cash-carrying crowd by passing on savings. Plus, if you pay in cash, you can stretch your dollar by avoiding any associated fees such as interest on a credit card balance or an ATM/debit card convenience fee.

Money talks, so let it scream volumes for you. Whenever making a major purchase, offer to pay for it using cash to strengthen your bargaining power when asking for a lower price. Remember, take the initiative! Your ability to pay in cash saves the seller money, which they can pass along to you in the form of a discount.

The power of paying in cash isn't limited to purchasing *things*. If you don't have health insurance for a specific issue (such as chiropractic or dental), paying your fees in cash (or check) can often get you a lower price. Many gas stations even offer a special price for cash-paying customers.

Cutting Costs with Coupons

I know coupon-cutting can feel like a painful bore, but it can enable you to buy twice as much for the same amount of money. But even if you can't bear cutting coupons, I'll tell you how you can get someone else to do the work for you!

A wise coupon-wielding shopper can rack up substantial savings by using multiple coupons on a single item, if the store allows it. If there's a sale price on top of that, you just saved more money!

What are you waiting for? Grab an envelope, a pair of scissors, and a can-do attitude, and let's start clipping—and in some cases, clicking!

Where to Find Coupons

Think the Sunday paper is the only place to get coupons? Think again. While coupons are nothing new, there are many creative ways to use them and to acquire them in the first place.

For example, consider using a coupon-clipping service. It's illegal to sell coupons, but it's perfectly legal to pay someone for their time and effort to collect, clip, and organize them for you. Using such a service enables you to purchase only the coupons you'll use for a nominal fee. Not only do you save the time and effort by not having to find and clip the coupons yourself, but you're guaranteed to only get the coupons you'll actually use. (For more on coupon-clipping services, see Resources.)

The backs of cash register receipts are another great place to find coupons toward dining out, dry-cleaning bills, and even car maintenance. If you know ahead of time there's a valuable coupon on the back of the cash register tape and you have a friendly cashier, ask him to scroll out an extra length of the tape so you can get more coupons.

 Super Saver

Keep your coupons where you'll use them—with you! Using an envelope inside your purse or wallet, organize coupons by expiration date with the most current one on top to ensure a valuable coupon doesn't get lost in the mix before you get to use it.

You can also go directly to the source—the manufacturer—for coupons. If you like a product, let the manufacturer know and ask for coupons. Many manufacturers have a toll-free "tell us what you think" line or at the very least a customer service phone number you can call or an e-mail address you can write to. When you do, be sure to ask for coupons so you can continue purchasing their products. They're grateful for the repeat business, and you can reap the savings.

> **Dollar $tretcher**
>
> Often store employees can give you a heads-up on an upcoming sales or clearance markdowns before they're advertised. If you have a specific purchase in mind, ask an employee.

Nowadays, you can do nearly everything from your computer—purchase and print airline tickets or postage and even click and print coupons. Although some stores have placed restrictions on printable coupons use due to fraudulent activity, more and more stores are embracing the practice. From promotional coupons on manufacturer web pages to entire sites devoted to these money-savers, printable coupons are essential in a dollar stretcher's arsenal of tools. (For a list of printable coupon sites, check out Resources.)

How to Use Coupons

Your mother probably continually told you to be nice, and standing in a cash register line is a great place to put this into practice—especially if you forgot your store-issued coupons at home. Nine times out of ten, the cashier will ask how you are, so tell her and then remember to reciprocate. After all, cashiers are people, too. Be nice to her, and she'll likely be nice to you and probably even identify with your predicament. She may have the same coupon available for you to use then and there or be able to tell you how to get another one.

If you live in a part of the country where stores permit coupon doubling, take advantage. If you don't, you can still use coupons to compound your savings even more. Many coupons have "No Doubling" printed across the top, but that doesn't prevent you from using a manufacturer's coupon in conjunction with a store coupon or a sale price. You can even use coupons on clearance or discount items to bring the cost down even more.

Spending money is as much about knowing how to play the game as it is about actually purchasing an item. From the background music in stores to the specifics of product packaging and placement, manufacturers, stores, and advertisers know how to play the game. It's time you did, too. The next time you enter the marketplace to make a purchase, whether it be in person or online, be sure you're prepared to win by knowing how to spend. After all, it's your money at stake!

Penny Pitfall

While at the cash register, keep an eye out for incorrect prices, duplicate product scans, and any extra weight unnecessarily added to the scale when purchasing produce. It might not save you much money, but it will help protect you from accidentally paying for something you didn't buy.

Chapter 2

When to Spend Your Money

In This Chapter

- ◆ Stock up and save
- ◆ Buy according to your schedule, not theirs
- ◆ Best time of day, week, and year for deals
- ◆ When *not* to shop to save

You've probably heard the saying, "Strike while the iron's hot." Well, that applies to spending money, too. Timing is everything when it comes to getting more for your hard-earned cash because you can stretch your dollar by planning *when* to spend your money.

In this chapter, you learn when to spend and when to wait to get more bang for your buck. After all, your goal is to keep more of those bucks in your pocket!

Stockpile When There's Savings

Many people today are "need buyers"—they buy something when they're of out it or when they have a need for it. Unfortunately, that's not the stretch-savvy way to spend. Waiting until you're in need leaves you at the mercy of the seller. And the more badly you need something, the more willing you are to pay a higher price. Take the power away from merchants, and instead begin purchasing items when the price is right *for you*. This means you have to learn how to stockpile.

Stockpiling sets you up for dollar-stretching success as well as convenience. You'll encounter less frustration as you'll likely have extras on hand when you need them, and you'll save time and effort by minimizing trips to the store.

The challenge with stocking up is knowing where to put everything you buy. A bit of creativity can help here. Put every closet, corner, nook, and cranny in your home to work for you. When you realize the vast savings and convenience that can be yours, you won't think twice about reinventing storage possibilities around your home.

Following Sales Cycles

But before you go out and stock up and save, wait a second. There really can be *too* much of a good thing, including extra stuff at home, no matter how useful and how great of a deal you got. After all, you don't want to be tripping over toilet paper for the next 4 years, do you?

The key is to purchase just enough to get you through to the next discount opportunity. And like anything else, there are tricks to this trade. Become a sales-cycle sleuth, and you'll never have to pay full price again.

Uncovering sales timetables isn't difficult. Start watching sales fliers and coupon circulars in your area for repetition and patterns to anticipate when you'll best be able to snag a deal. Even if you don't crack open the sales fliers past the front page, look to the *loss leaders* to determine what you can purchase that week for the most value.

When you've discovered a pattern, create a sales-cycle tracking method in a notebook or on a calendar so you'll know when to keep your eyes open for particular items. When an item goes on sale, mark the date so you'll be able to anticipate the next sale. In general, sales cycles are 9 weeks long. Use that as a starting point to determine the cycle lengths specific to the stores you shop most often. This helps you not only anticipate your next opportunity to stock up at a savings, but also determine how much you should purchase during any one sales period. It shouldn't take you long to master this cycle so another deal comes around just when you're running out of your stocked goods.

def•i•ni•tion

A **loss leader** is an item advertised, usually on the front page of a sales flier, at a sale price that's actually below cost. Advertisers use these items to lure you into the store and bank on you buying other, more expensive products while you're there.

Stockpiling Tips

Lack of storage space isn't the only challenge stocking up can present. If you're not accustomed to "shopping" from inventory you already have at home, you can easily forget what you have and head out to purchase more.

To avoid this, assign a set place to store and organize your purchases. It also helps, at least in the beginning, to keep a record of what's stored where. Keep this list in a place that's handy for everyone in the house to reference, such as on the refrigerator or inside a frequently used cabinet door. Plus, a list is nicer to look at than a lot of cluttered goods, so tuck away the merchandise and keep out the list for reference.

Be mindful of expiration dates, and I don't just mean those on food items. You might be tempted to stock up on items such as antiperspirants, over-the-counter drugs, and toothpaste when there's a great sale—after all, these types of purchases can reap the biggest savings. But don't purchase so much that your supply is in danger of expiring before you can use it. Check expiration dates when you make the purchase, and carefully rotate your stock at home so you use the items due to expire sooner first.

Super Saver

Keep a permanent marker handy to number your purchases in order of what should be used first, or plainly note the expiration date so it's easy to read.

Time Your Purchases to Get Quality

Stretching your dollar isn't just about saving money. After all, what good is purchasing something if it's of poor quality? Time your purchases so you're able to get the best possible combination of savings and quality. Whether you're buying bananas or clothing basics, both where and when matter.

Shop on the Store's Schedule

Who you know can really help you save. Get to know the employees at your local stores, and ask the managers what time deliveries come in and when the products are out on the shelves. You'll be able to get the best selection and increase the likelihood that a sale product will be on the shelf when you want it.

 Super Saver

> If you're at the store during a sale only to find the item you want out of stock, ask for a rain check that will enable you to purchase the quantity you want later at the current sale price.

Take in-store bakeries, for example. These can be as much of an advantage as they can be a money-waster. Sure, nothing's yummier than fresh-baked bread, but remember that most bakery items are free of the preservatives packaged items contain. As a result, the fresh stuff can get stale and develop mold more quickly. Ensure a longer shelf life by purchasing bread and baked goods as close to when they come out of the oven as possible. Getting to know the bakery employees means you'll get to know their baking schedule as well as when they may discount day-old items for a quick sale, giving you first crack at clearance baked goods.

When to Get the Best Deal on Fresh Food

It's hard to beat the flavor of fresh produce, but fresh fruits and vegetables lose nutrients and overall quality the longer they sit on the store shelf. If you shop at a traditional grocery store for your fresh fruits and vegetables, be sure to frequent a store that has a high produce turnover rate. Such a store is more likely to have fresher fruit on its shelves.

And don't forget to make friends with the produce department employees. They can tip you off to when deliveries arrive, providing you the opportunity to get first pick. Another great thing about getting to know the produce department employees is that, if they know you're a frequent shopper, they're more likely to oblige when you ask for a sample of new produce prior to committing to a purchase so you don't buy something that's no good or you don't like. (Don't graze on your own, though!)

Fresh produce can account for a good portion of a grocery bill, so be sure you only pay for quality. Try to purchase some items at the peak of ripeness to use now, and select some just a few days shy of being ripe to use later. You'll get more for your money by ensuring the produce is ready when you are, and not before. Plus, you can lengthen the time between visits to the store, and that alone can be a real time- and money-saver.

Plan When to Shop

If it's worth making a trip out to the store, it's worth planning time to do it right. Make plans to shop when you know you'll have enough time to devote to the process. Comparing prices and value takes time. So does getting through the checkout process and loading the car. There's only one thing worse than having to leave a store empty-handed because you ran out of time, and that's leaving the store with the wrong product at a bad price.

Dollar $tretcher

Use supply and demand to your advantage. If there's an excess of supply, use it to help you demand a better price. Take into consideration that the opposite can be true, too; don't wait too long to purchase something, or your own demand for it will have you paying any price to get it.

Calendar-Based Savings

Often the best time to get a great deal is when fewer people are shopping for it. Shopping off-season or right before the newest model or version comes out is often a money-saver. For example, purchase new cars, computers, and small electronics just before a new model comes out to take advantage of clearance prices. The only exception to this rule is fresh produce. Nature's abundance often ensures there's more supply than demand, keeping prices low and quality high.

Shopping during other times—times not so easily categorized—can help ensure the deepest discounts and the best deals. It may not always be practical or even possible, but if you can time major appliance purchases for a holiday weekend, you'll be able to take advantage of the deep discounts offered by short-term sale prices. Sometimes it can even pay to put the cart before the horse: shopping during pregnancy, for example, can be an ideal time to look around for baby necessities and get the best prices. You'll have months to be extra selective while waiting for the lowest possible prices—and your new little one!

> **Super Saver**
>
> You can find great deals on luxury items and most large-ticket purchases during hard economic times because fewer people have the discretionary money to spend on them.

The time of year, day of week, and even time of day can affect how much you pay for items. While it can pay off to keep an eye on any trends in your area, the following information can also help you get the best deal.

Many people save shopping for when it's most convenient for them, but that won't always pay off with the best price. Be willing to change around your shopping schedule, and you'll be more likely to snag a great deal, as the following list shows:

Month of the Year	What to Buy
January	Bicycles, sports equipment, furniture
February	Electronics (TVs, computers, MP3 players, etc.)

March	Winter coats, winter clothing
April	Cookware
May	Cookware
June	Electronics, furniture
July	Computers, furniture
August	Office/school supplies
September	Cars, summer clothing
October	Trees, shrubs, cookware
November	Cookware, wedding dresses
December	Champagne, new cars

There really is no steadfast rule as to which day of the week is best for shopping. However, history proves that some days are better than others. Use this list to increase your chances for getting the most from your dollar, no matter what day of the week:

Day of the Week	What to Buy
Sunday	Groceries
Monday	Cars
Tuesday	Groceries
Wednesday	Airline tickets
Thursday	Books
Friday	Nothing (unless it's Black Friday)
Saturday	Anything you anticipate going on sale Sunday (Some stores already have Sunday's sale items discounted by Saturday evening.)

Don't forget to look at your watch to get the best deal, too. Time of day can have a great affect on not just how much you pay, but what kind of value you get as well, as the following list shows:

Time of Day	What to Buy
Morning	Gas, haircut, salon services (Any service you pay for will generally be a better value in the morning because the person providing the service will likely be less tired versus later in the day.)
Afternoon	Shoes (Feet often swell during the afternoon hours. Purchasing shoes in the afternoon ensures a more comfortable fit.)
Evening	Cars
Night	Airline tickets (Airlines usually release unbooked seats around midnight. These seats are often discounted to ensure a full flight.)

Adjusting your spending to a timetable other than just convenience can help you cash into big savings and better value. So arm yourself with a calendar and your watch, and watch how far your collar can stretch!

When to Shop at Thrift Stores

Anyone who's shopped at secondhand stores knows that what you find is often a matter of luck. You can, however, improve your odds of getting good-quality items by visiting thrift stores early in the week. The vast majority of people make donations during the weekend, and the new stock is then sorted, priced, and placed on the shelves during the first few days of the week. Cheers to Secondhand Mondays!

You don't have to wait for donations to be priced to make a purchase. If you see an item being donated that you're interested in, don't wait. Ask to speak to a manager to have the item priced on the spot so you can be the first to snatch it up. If the manager is unwilling to give you a price for the item then and there, ask if you may leave your phone number and have the item placed on hold for you to purchase later after it's been priced.

When to Break for Garage Sales

For the best selection at garage sales, visit early in the morning. But for the best prices, visit late in the day when sellers are more likely to lower their prices to make a quick sale.

Be sure to take an adventurous spirit with you, too. While you may not be able to dicker over price at thrift stores, it's acceptable and often expected at garage sales. Always speak up and ask if a seller will accept a lower price for an item. Buying in bulk at garage sales can also help you save. If you'll be purchasing multiple items, wait and ask the seller if she'd take a discounted price for the entire lot.

Penny Pitfall

If you're going to garage sales with a wad of cash on you, conceal your money. If you pull out your money to make the point that you're a serious buyer, organize your bills with the smallest bills facing out. Advertising how much money you have to spend certainly doesn't help you get the best price.

When *Not* to Shop

As important as knowing when to shop is knowing when to steer clear of spending your money. For example, never go food shopping when you're hungry. You'll fill that cart so fast with stuff you don't need your wallet won't know what hit it when you get to the checkout line!

The same reasoning applies to not shopping when you're sad or depressed. Not only are you more likely to pay higher prices if you're down in the dumps, but you're more likely to purchase items just to soothe your aching spirit. Shop when you have a purpose, not as a means of "retail therapy."

If you must shop when you're hungry, buy a small snack to graze on while you're shopping. Keeping your hunger pains at bay helps you buy less overall and keeps your total bill in check. For a quick, inexpensive snack, stop by the deli and purchase a slice or two of cold cuts or cheese. While there, ask for a complimentary water as well. This protein-packed snack is not only inexpensive and convenient, but it'll give you an energy boost to get your shopping done and is a cheap insurance policy against unnecessary purchases ending up in your cart.

Shopping when you're tired can have negative consequences as well. If your energy is lagging, you're less likely to compare prices and much more likely to simply grab what's easiest and quickest. To avoid sabotaging your savings, schedule your shopping for a time when you'll be more alert and able to focus. Even if that means shopping in the middle of the night, you'll be more likely to get more for your money and pay less overall. More and more stores are open 24 hours a day or have extended hours. Of course, you can shop from the comfort of home online at any hour of the day or night.

Any time is a good time to save money and stretch your dollar. Make it happen by shopping on your own schedule while knowing when to best take advantage of fluctuations in pricing. Your efforts will be well rewarded.

Chapter 3

Where to Get More for Your Money

In This Chapter

- ◆ Beware product placement
- ◆ Locate the best prices
- ◆ Scout alternative shopping sources
- ◆ Eliminate the middleman
- ◆ Save money online

After reading Chapter 2, you now know when to shop. In this chapter, you learn where to shop. After all, being in the right place goes a long way toward stretching your dollar. Keep reading to discover the secrets of where to go to get more bang for your buck.

Dig a Bit for Better Value

You can find great deals at the stores you already shop. If you know where to look for bargains, you'll be sure to stretch your dollar quite a long way.

Stores don't advertise their best deals unless it's for the express purpose of getting you into the store to spend more money. Naturally, store managers would much rather you purchase full-price items. Think of looking for these deals as a treasure hunt. If it's worth finding, it'll likely require a little effort on your part. Put on your hunting gear, and let's go to work!

Don't Fall for Product Placement

In grocery stores, items are rotated on the shelves to ensure that the item closest to the front is also the item that expires first. When I worked in retail, this process was called "recovery." (I can't help but think the term refers to the store's efforts to recover possible lost sales shortly before the products go bad.)

Don't fall for this product placement. Get only top-quality for your dollar by taking the extra effort to select an item that's not directly in front. Your bags of chips are less likely to be full of crumbs, your bread won't get stale as quickly, and your bottle of lotion is less likely to have been used as a tester by curious shoppers before you.

> **Dollar $tretcher**
>
> When people change their mind on food items at the register, the items can end up sitting at room temperature for who knows how long. These items are later returned to the front of their shelves. Reach toward the back of the shelf to ensure the product you pay for has been properly stored at the right temperature.

Expand your treasure-hunting skills beyond just looking for clearance and discounted items. Seek bargains simply by looking in untraditional areas of the store. By thinking outside the box, you'll likely discover regular-priced items that are bargain priced every day due to their location in the store.

For example, are you looking for a spice? Get it cheaper in the bulk section or the ethnic food section. (Ethnic food sections of grocery stores often have a lot of great stuff at a portion of the price you might find it elsewhere.) Looking for towels, disposable or otherwise, or even a funnel? Head to the automotive section. Looking for good glue? Try the hardware section. You can increase your product selection and the likelihood of getting a great price if you're able to think beyond traditional product placement.

Product placement is purposefully tempting, too. Small toys are tucked into the cereal aisle to get kids to beg their parents to buy them. Kitchen utensils are placed on hanging strips throughout the baking aisle. Magazines are placed where you'll most likely be standing around waiting, giving you more time to read the headlines and increase the chances of you tossing them in your cart. By all means, use this type of product placement to help you remember to purchase something you might need, but travel to another area of the store where you're assured a better selection and can price-check the competition.

It doesn't stop there. Savvy shoppers know shelves at eye-level are prime real estate where brand-name and more expensive items are placed. If it's easier to see and easier to reach for, you can bet it probably won't be the best product to stretch your buck. There's one instance where the opposite can be true, however: name-brand cereal, often with a high sugar content, is usually placed on lower shelves to catch the eyes of kiddos passing by. Manufacturers are banking on your kiddo to beg you to buy it.

Where to Find Deals

Just as important as knowing what and where to avoid is knowing where in the store to turn for a deal. As a general rule of thumb, the farther back you travel in a store, the more likely you are to find better prices. Aisle endcaps are also common places to find discount bins.

Nothing ventured, nothing gained applies to shopping, too. Similar, more value-priced products are on store shelves right along with the pricier brands, but you may have to look a bit harder for them. Generic and store-brand items are usually placed on lower and top shelves. Look a bit harder and reach a bit farther to get these products for deeper discounts.

> **Dollar $tretcher**
>
> Skip buying gum and mints at the cash register. Buy them in the candy aisle instead, where you can purchase them bundled for less. When you buy them at the register, you pay for the convenience of purchasing one package at a time.

Often they're the same product, just packaged differently. Don't assume you're taking a gamble when purchasing generic products. Most come with a money-back satisfaction guarantee.

Know a Store's Strengths

If you're anything like me, you have different people you turn to in different situations. You call specific friends when you feel like a laugh and ring others when you need advice. Take this same approach to shopping, and you'll bank bigger savings. While driving all over town is obviously counterproductive, having a few different stores in your shopping repertoire broadens your horizons for better selection and increases your opportunities for savings.

One-stop shopping may be convenient, and it may even save you a few bucks on gas, but that convenience isn't necessarily cheap. Get to know the stores in your area to figure out which have the best prices on specific products. Grocery stores carry many products such as diapers and cosmetics as a courtesy to their customers—and price them accordingly. Discount stores, on the other hand, make it their goal to offer great prices on those same items and can do so by selling more of them. A willingness to shop at a few different stores can get you a mountain of purchases at molehill prices.

> **Dollar $tretcher**
>
> Many brick-and-mortar stores also have online stores, but they don't always offer the same deals. Not only is the selection different, but the prices—even for the same items—often differ as well. Many stores offer special web-only pricing to solicit more online business.

Not Just Groceries Anymore

Like almost everything else, grocery stores are getting bigger and bigger and offering more services than just groceries. Take advantage of this!

For example, many grocery stores have bulk food sections. Usually, these bulk items are sold by weight and with less packaging, which means a substantial savings for you. Some of the best bulk savings can be had on items such as herbs and spices, dried beans, and nuts. To get the best value for your bulk buying dollar, purchase only from stores that have a high turnover rate to ensure you're getting the freshest supply possible.

Sure, ordering a wedding cake from a grocery store may be a bit unconventional, for example, but it can also save you some cash. Many in-store bakeries rival the quality of professional bakeries at a substantially lower cost, and most have at least one professional cake decorator on staff. Check out their services and work, just as you would any place else. They most likely will gladly accommodate by providing samples as well as photographs of their previous work.

Consider taking advantage of your grocery store's deli to cater an event. You'll be able to enjoy the ease of having someone else do all the prep work and cooking while still saving a substantial amount of money compared to professional catering. Many stores make it even easier for you to save money by offering discounted volume pricing for larger groups. Inquire at your store's deli counter for more information.

The next time you don't feel like making dinner, turn to the grocery store. More and more grocery stores can make eating at home as convenient as eating out, but for a fraction of the cost. From ready-to-eat gourmet salads in the deli case, to rotisserie chickens hot and ready to go, to ethnic entrées, the quality can rival that of restaurants. Plus, you can pick and choose for more variety and to suit everyone's tastes. You'll pay substantially less by dining in on grocery store takeout than you would dining at a sit-down restaurant. The money you save on dining out and tipping can be stretched for different kinds of family fun!

Price Matching

Stores that offer price matching or lowest-price guarantees have a huge edge over the competition and can provide you with big savings. You'll have to keep your eyes open for a better price elsewhere and be prepared to support the claim, but you can get the best value for your dollar by requesting that the lower price be honored either at the time you purchase or after the fact.

Some stores are so confident in their ability to provide the best price that they offer 110 percent price guarantees. They'll not only honor the lower price, but they'll give you an additional 10 percent off.

Extra Benefits

Needless to say, you work hard for your money. It makes sense to shop at stores that work equally hard to protect it. Do just that by frequenting stores willing to stand behind the stock they carry and the subsequent purchases you make. Should anything ever go awry, you'll thank yourself for having purchased from a store that offers additional guarantees and longer return or exchange periods. Shopping at such a store can help get what you pay for over the long haul.

Some stores even offer receipt lookup in the event you need to return an item and don't have the receipt. By scanning an item's *UPC* code and the method you likely used for payment (credit card, debit card, or even your checking account), the store is able to locate the purchase if it was made during a certain time period and you can get your money back. Shopping at such a store is like getting a free insurance policy to protect the value of your purchasing dollars.

def•i•ni•tion

UPCs (universal product codes) are bar codes used to scan item prices and help track inventory. You can even search online for a UPC to do price checks and locate sellers near you. An easy way to do this is to visit google.com and search for a UPC number. You'll get back everything from a simple description of the specific product to various purchase locations.

Alternative Shopping Sources

If you're willing to explore alternative shopping sources, you'll likely see a great financial return on your efforts. Tried-and-true shopping sources may take consumer business for granted, but online sellers and newer businesses often work harder to garnish customer loyalty. Use this to your advantage.

Outlet and Thrift Stores

Outlet stores (sometimes called factory stores) are a great place to stretch your dollar. Outlets are filled with overstocked merchandise that didn't sell in the retail stores, as well as items that couldn't be sold at full price due to a variety of cosmetic flaws. Cosmetic flaws only affect the appearance of an item, not how well it functions, so if you're willing to overlook a small dent, scratch, or a slightly crooked seam, you could see substantial savings in your bill.

Outlet and thrift stores aren't reserved for clothing and housewares. Bakery thrift stores are popping up in communities across the country. Regular stores may not be able to sell baked goods near or past their pull date, but thrift stores can. You may not have as much time to use the product, but you'll only pay a fraction of the retail price.

Manufacturer Direct

You can expand your shopping options by purchasing directly from a manufacturer. Cutting out the middleman can help cut the cost for the same products you find in the big box stores. Although there might be a minimum purchase requirement, the price you pay per item or unit will be significantly lower.

Beyond price, sometimes the only difference between purchasing from a manufacturer versus a retailer is the shopping experience itself. If you're willing to forego a fancy shopping experience or a decked-out showroom, you'll likely benefit from a deep discount. Consider buying manufacturer-direct when you're in the market for big-ticket items such as furniture and home remodeling supplies. Computer hardware and software purchased *OEM* can be snagged at a significantly lower price, too.

def•i•ni•tion

OEM stands for "original equipment manufacturer" and describes a product being sold bare-bones without any fancy packaging, manuals, or supporting materials.

Warehouse Clubs

Warehouse clubs are a great way to stretch your dollar. After paying a membership fee, you can purchase products in bulk, lowering the cost per item. Many warehouse stores also have their own store brand for various items that meet or exceed national standards and are available at even greater savings.

Penny Pitfall

Warehouse clubs can be a great way to stock up at a savings, but resist the urge to buy more than you need or can use before they expire.

To get the maximum value for your dollar, be sure your savings over the course of the year exceeds the amount you paid to join in the first place.

Watch-and-Shop Options

Home shopping is not only easy, but it can offer great value as well. The two main home shopping options are QVC (Quality, Value, Convenience) and HSN (Home Shopping Network).

The biggest opportunity for value combined with a great price is each network's special deal of the day. QVC calls it "Today's Special Value," and HSN calls it "Today's Special." Whatever it's called, you can bet it'll be a great product at an even better price. Another benefit of shopping one of these networks is the flexible payment options. QVC refers to it as "Easy Pay," and HSN calls it "Flexpay," but both offer the flexibility of paying for the purchase over time without accruing interest on your credit card.

If you don't want to be chained to the TV or place your order via the phone, you can access the same purchasing opportunities (and more) at their websites as well: www.qvc.com and www.hsn.com.

def•i•ni•tion

Infomercial is a cross between two words, *information* and *commercial,* and is used to describe television programming specifically aired to sell a product that is usually not available in stores.

Infomercials are another watch-and-shop option that seem to offer great value, but whether or not they actually do is questionable. A better bet is to save your money and wait for the item to eventually show up in stores or on a reputable shopping network that has an easy return policy.

Online Savings

How did we ever survive without the Internet? It has certainly changed the way we shop—as well as how we save. If you have a credit or debit card, a computer, and Internet access, you can shop the world without ever leaving home. And thankfully, with this new way to shop comes new ways to stretch your dollar.

Just as you can shop and buy with a point and a click, so can you price check in just a moment's time. Online shopping is not just convenient, but you also have an exhaustive amount of shopping sites to choose from, increasing the chances of finding a rock-bottom price. Use any search engine window to run a search on the item itself or take advantage of the help provided by any one of the number of price comparison sites available. (For a list of these sites, see Resources.)

The savings of outlet stores isn't reserved for only the brick-and-mortar type, as you'll see if you shop one of the many online outlets. (For a list of these, see Resources.) Word to the money wise: be sure the savings you score on the price isn't eaten up by the cost of shipping and handling.

Shop online when you need to find a specific item or you want more variety to choose from. Not only will you be able to shop the site of a store down the street but also one that's based halfway around the world.

 Super Saver _____

Protect yourself from identity theft by only entering personal information, including credit card numbers, on sites that feature the added protection of a secure socket layer (SSL). This encrypts your information for safer transmission online. Before entering and sending your payment information, look for *https* at the beginning of the site address.

Online merchants are sensitive to the hesitation of potential customers to make the leap to online shopping. On top of that, they're eager to lure customers from their competitors' sites. Many offer introductory or first-time-customer discounts to accomplish both of these goals. You not only stand to get a great price, but you can compound your savings by taking advantage of such an offer.

Discounts, Promotions, and Coupon Codes

If you like the idea reaping the savings of coupons without clipping a single one, keep reading. These little paper cost-cutters aren't reserved for stores of the traditional variety; they've gone virtual, too. Instead of paper and scissors, these require a point and click.

Before committing to any purchase online, look for a promotional code. These are usually a combination of numbers and letters that automatically provide some kind of discount when they're used at the time of purchase. Open a browser window and search for "coupon code" or "discount code" and the name of the site you're making the purchase from. Then, just copy and paste the promotional code to the checkout page. Many sites devoted to coupon savings in general also feature sections on online promotional codes. (For more information, check out Resources.)

You may be able to compound your virtual coupon savings by using more than one code at a time. For example, depending on the merchant's policies, you may be able to use one promotional code for a discount off your total purchase amount and another code to discount or completely eliminate shipping costs.

Other Ways to Save Online

If you're looking for a hard-to-find item or simply a great deal, you can try your luck at the online auction site eBay. Almost everything imaginable is available there, and because sellers set their own prices, much can be snagged for a song.

Another great site for phenomenal deals is Craigslist.org. Individuals post their wares for sale (or even for free); however, unlike eBay, Craigslist is *not* an auction site. It's an online community forum for everything from general information to personals to items for sale. All communication is done via e-mail directly with the seller, and because each Craigslist site is region- or city-specific, everyone is local and there are no additional shipping fees to pay. Be brave enough to ask for a lower price, though. You may just be rewarded.

The person who said, "You don't get anything for free," clearly never visited www.freecycle.org. If you're in need of something and don't mind acquiring it secondhand, check out this site before shelling out any money. From appliances to furniture, you can often find it on freecycle for free. Site membership is completely free, and members can also feel good about doing their part to lighten the load on landfills, too.

Another way to save with online shopping is by shopping stores located outside your home state. You're only required to pay sales tax on purchases made from businesses located in the same state, so save money by avoiding paying tax altogether.

A big drawback to shopping online is the shipping and handling charges. However, there are ways to minimize or completely eliminate these. Some larger merchants that have both traditional store locations as well as online stores offer a ship-to-store option. By picking up your order at a store location near you, you can avoid paying shipping and handling fees. And some online merchants waive the shipping and handling fee if your total purchase exceeds a set dollar amount. Still others offer free shipping as a service to new customers. Often, though, you may be able to secure a better price even with the additional costs included simply because you're able to cast your deal-seeking net wider.

Even if the additional cost of shipping and handling seems high, don't make the assumption that shopping online isn't worth your while. You could very well be letting a great deal get away.

Dollar $tretcher

If you're purchasing a gift online to send to someone, take advantage of using a different billing and shipping address. Even if you have to pay a fee for gift wrapping service, it's likely cheaper than shipping the item to yourself, wrapping it, and then paying to ship the package to the recipient.

No one *owes* you a good deal, so get caught up in the thrill of the hunt and score yourself a great deal. There's nothing like the rush of adrenaline and the savings in your wallet to keep you motivated. So go out, look around, and stretch your dollar!

Chapter 4

What to Do to Stretch Your Dollar

In This Chapter

♦ Smart spending means more for less

♦ Prioritizing your *wants* versus *needs* spending

♦ DIY (do it yourself) and SYD (stretch your dollar)

♦ Make commission-based purchases work for you

♦ More for you, less for Uncle Sam

♦ When it's okay to pay more … and when it's not

Especially in hard economic times, you'll likely do everything possible to stretch your dollar. The good news is that there's so much you can do! The first step is to have an open mind and be open to new things. You can still have the things you want; you just have to work a little harder to get them. Try a few of the suggestions in this chapter, or try them all, but remember that the amount of effort you apply is proportional to the amount of dollar-stretching success you'll see.

So get ready, get set, and go *do* everything you can to realize more bang for your buck.

Stretch-Smart Practices

Over the years, I've figured out that it's not how hard you work or even how much money you earn; it's how smart you are about spending and using what you have. By getting wiser about making spending decisions and how you use what you purchase, you can make your money stretch farther.

Your Wants Versus Needs

One of the first things you learn in any book on personal finance is that you need to identify the difference between *needs* and *wants*. That applies in this book, too, because the easiest route to stretching your dollar is to simply stop spending on those wants. Unfortunately, though, life without those wants can be incredibly boring, and besides, the whole point of learning to stretch your dollar is not to have to change your lifestyle to keep more dough in your pocket.

There are no "right" or "wrong" ways to spend money. And more often than not, it's those wants that make our lives more enjoyable and fulfilling. Instead of nixing spending on what you want altogether, prioritize your spending. Make the choice to tighten your spending belt in some areas, and you can spend more freely in others. Spending styles are as unique as the individuals doing the spending. By acknowledging your spending weaknesses and ridding yourself of any accompanying guilt, you free yourself to find spending, saving, and stretching solutions that are much more likely to stick. Crash diets don't work; neither do spending or debt diets. Make real, lasting change. Decide what's most important to you, and make allowances for that spending.

Sometimes the best way to stop reaching for your wallet is to reach for something you already have. Respect your prior purchase choices by approaching them more positively, and you'll likely be able to discover solutions you didn't know were there. Think there's nothing to eat at home? Search online for the few ingredients you *do* have in your pantry and the word *recipe* to discover new ways to whip up something.

Lamenting how small your home is? Maximize the space you do have in innovative ways. Wish you had a new car? Focus on the big car payment you don't have and the spending freedom your current car affords you.

Don't Do as You're Told

Advertising is everywhere, trying to tell you what to do with your money. From catchy little jingles to small subliminal visuals, every day we're bombarded with ads that try to tell us to buy, buy, buy. It can be hard to resist. But resist you must. Build up a resistance to these seductive, enticing, delicious, life-enhancing … *lies!* This is hard to do, so you'll have to be smart. The key is to start small.

My grandpa used to say, "Fool me once, shame on you. Fool me twice, shame on me." That little phrase resonates whenever I make a purchase or read a set of directions. You should remember that, too. After all, almost everyone is out to make money (including you and me). Everyone is trying to make their product seem like a must-have. *This product will make you beautiful! This one will save your life! This one will make your husband love you more!* Resist these ads, and make the most of what you have on hand before looking for new stuff to add to your probably already-overstocked life. Remember, advertising's sole purpose is to make your feel dissatisfied so you'll buy more stuff!

For example, don't follow directions. Make products you purchase last longer by figuring out for yourself how much to use to get the desired result. More often than not, product directions instruct you to use more than you actually have to so you'll use up the project more quickly and buy more often. You can usually get the same results and make your money stretch simply by using less than you're told to use. Do *not* lather, rinse, and repeat. Just lather and rinse.

Don't wash in warm or hot water unless something needs to be sanitized. Most laundered items get just as clean with cold water and actually look nicer, longer because the colors don't run or fade in cold water. You'll also save money on your energy bill by not having to heat the water.

Avoid the "use once, throw away" mind-set, and use something twice (or more, if you can) before tossing it. Many items have enough life left in them for more than one use, which means you can get double for your money. Turn over printed paper and print on the other side. Use disposable razors, flatware, and straws more than once. Prioritize the use of a paper towel so you can use it more than once. For example, use it to dry off the counter first and then wipe off Fido's paws when he comes in from the rain.

Skip name-brand refills or accessories when possible. It's important to remember that not using a name-brand component in some electronics can void a warranty, but it's even more important to remember that sometimes it doesn't matter all. Your vacuum isn't going to know if you're using name-brand bags or not, but your bank account will. Take a look at the ingredients of your favorite shampoo and then take a look at the generic equivalent. You probably won't see much difference in the two!

Don't buy another bottle when yours is empty. Whenever possible, opt for the larger container of concentrate or refill, and reuse your original bottle at home. You'll save money, and you'll help save the planet from excessive waste.

 Super Saver _____

When you can, reuse items rather than tossing them after they've served their initial purpose. Used dryer sheets make great dusting and floor-cleaning cloths. Cut off the top portion of a plastic beverage bottle to make a funnel. Use mesh produce bags as household cleaning scrubbers. Wrap strands of lights or electrical cords around empty paper towel rolls for easy organizing and storage rather than purchasing another tool for this purpose.

Make different sections of the grocery store multitask for you. For example, don't assume the deli counter is just for deli purchases. Select a large block of cheese or ham from the cold case and take it to the deli to have it sliced for the same convenience at a smaller price.

Don't let a product sit for the amount of time the package directions say—let it sit *longer* to get better results. *Caveat:* of course, be careful that doing so won't actually cause damage; look for this warning on the package. But if it's safe, you can often get the same great results with less amount of product if you're willing to be a bit patient and give it more time to work. Household cleaners, stain removers, and even plain old dish soap all work better—even with less product—if you allow them more time to do their job.

Stop worrying so much about what you spend your money on and, instead, start focusing on how to make what you do buy last longer. You'll keep your dollars longer in your wallet as well!

Commission-Based Purchases

A commission-based salesperson's paycheck depends in part on the number of sales she makes. While this can sometimes lead to a high-pressure shopping experience, you can also leverage this opportunity for great savings. In any buying situation—especially this one—it helps to remind yourself that you're the one in the position of power. Refuse to be pressured or intimidated. After all, you're the customer. You're always right.

Listen to Save

If only saving money were as easy as doing nothing. Well, this tip comes close: be silent and let the salesperson talk. He'll likely have some spiel to share with you about why you should buy what and why you should buy from him.

Such a sales situation is much like a game of poker; don't prematurely show all your cards by asking too many questions upfront. You may be able to learn more about his sales position if you're willing to let him talk long enough. Is he desperate for a sale? Is he worried about not making his quota? The more you know about him and the company, the better equipped you are to haggle successfully. You won't know if you're too busy monopolizing the conversation.

Call His Bluff to Save

Know when to walk away, or at least pretend to do so. If you want a deal, be willing to walk away. It may be your goal to make a purchase at the best price, but it's the salesperson's goal to simply make a sale.

He'll likely do everything in his power to keep you from walking away, so use that to your advantage to leverage a better price. He'll undoubtedly start at a higher price to gain a larger commission, but in the end, he knows any sale is better than no sale.

> **Dollar $tretcher**
>
> If a salesperson gives you great deal, ask for the salesperson's business card, and share that information with your friends. You may even get a referral program kickback if a friend takes advantage of a great deal, too.

If the salesperson is too aggressive, you might want to walk away for real. An overly aggressive sales associate is a sure sign of desperation, and there's probably a very good reason he's not getting the sales. Walk away now to protect your money.

Haggle to Save

Haggling is often part of the money-saving game, but still, start small when you ask for a particular price. You may very well be willing and able to spend more, but if you want to walk out with the price you want, start low. Begin by offering 40 to 50 percent *less* than what you're actually willing to pay. The sales associate might scoff at you. Let him. It's part of the game. Have your poker face on, and let the price move up from there.

Even if you don't know what you're talking about, do your best to exude confidence when you're haggling. You may not know everything there is to know about the purchase, but at the very least you should know exactly what you *want* to purchase and how much you're willing to pay. The more confident you seem, the less easy it is for the salesperson to take advantage of you and your wallet.

Aside from securing a great price, you can also haggle for extras to be *comped*. Depending on whether it's an appliance, a car, or furniture, you can haggle over delivery, haul-away, setup, oil changes, or even ongoing car washes. These additional services are likely things you would have to pay for anyway and can add extra value to your purchase.

> **def•i•ni•tion**
>
> **Comped** is another way to say "complimentary." If something is comped, any associated fee (or portion of a fee) is waived.

Do More Yourself

As the saying goes, time is money. And let's face it, so is a skill set. Whether it's a product or a service, every time you opt *not* do something yourself, you have to pay for it. This isn't necessarily a bad thing, though. After all, anyone who works a job and runs a household knows that sometimes it's more economical to pay for a little convenience than to lose your sanity. On the other hand, anyone looking to stretch his or her dollar can easily see results by keeping this in mind and making spending decisions accordingly.

When purchasing products, the more processed, packaged, or convenient something is, generally the higher the price. Be willing to do a bit more for yourself, and you can often find a direct correlation to the savings you'll see. If you're willing to bag your own groceries, you can stretch your dollar by shopping at a store that doesn't employ baggers. Use your own spray bottle, and you can purchase concentrate and dilute your own cleaners for less. Purchasing furniture that needs to be assembled is not only cheaper to purchase, but is less expensive and easier to transport, too.

Don't necessarily forgo all more expensive products, though. Stretching your dollars is also about improving your quality of life, so prioritize the convenience items you purchase. By making some concessions on others, you'll be better able to purchase the products that really do improve your life. For example, I don't mind washing and cutting up lettuce, so I'll rarely purchase bagged, prewashed greens. On the other hand, I hate spending time cleaning house, so disposable cleaning wipes are worth every last cent I spend on them.

Dollar $tretcher

Create your own convenience items to save time and money. Prep your own lettuce ahead of time and store in large resealable plastic bags. (Tuck a paper towel inside to wick away moisture and prolong its life.) Create your own premixed seasoning blends for ease of use and affordability. Check out Chapter 13 for more do-it-yourself convenience items that are green for the environment and keep more green in your pocket.

Increasing Your DIY Know-How

If you're looking to repair, replace, or remodel something, you're likely looking at a big bill, right? Not necessarily. With the Internet, a free education is only a few clicks away. Bribe experienced friends and family to help you with a project. Many hardware stores even offer free *DIY* classes to encourage purchases at their stores. Even if your local hardware store doesn't, chances are it's filled with helpful, knowledgeable employees who will gladly give you a quick crash course in whatever it is you need to do.

def·i·ni·tion

DIY stands for "do it yourself" and usually refers to home improvement, repair, or other jobs you can do without hiring a professional.

Your television is another great resource for free DIY training. Countless shows and even entire channels are devoted just to this topic and can make even complicated tasks seem less daunting. Many of these shows and networks also have accompanying websites that feature step-by-step, printable directions geared directly toward those with little to no experience.

If you ever do get to a point when it's necessary to call in an expert, don't miss out on a great learning opportunity. You're paying for their time, so stick around to watch and ask a few questions. You'll be able to pick up some of their techniques and get more value for your money by learning a thing or two.

Don't forget, too, that many professionals offer discounts specifically to entice new customers. Before you enlist their services, be sure to check out their website for any printable coupons or simply ask if there are any such discounts over the phone when you call to make an appointment. Many times such discounts exist but aren't necessarily advertised to all customers.

Stocking Your DIY Tool Chest

Sometimes it isn't just the know-how that's needed, but the right tools, too. Ensure success by equipping yourself with the best tools to do the job. For example, purchase a quality set of hair clippers and become an in-house hairdresser for all the men in the family. Or invest in a quality sewing machine to make easy work of altering hems and repairing clothing. Often all that's need is an adventurous spirit, a few parts, and the right tools to make many challenges successful and profitable. You may have to shell out some cash upfront to buy the tools, but the right tools are an investment in stretching your dollar over the long haul. Let's look at some DIY tool ideas:

Energy-efficient appliances. These may cost more upfront, but they'll cost less to run, saving you money over the life of the appliance.

Faucet aerator. Lower your water bill by using less water with the use of this little gadget.

Low-flow showerhead. Don't assume you have to give up water pressure to save water in the shower. You can find several water-saving showerheads on the market geared directly at counteracting this problem.

Programmable thermostat. This helps you maintain your home at a constant, comfortable temperature, and avoid the costly need to move the thermostat up and down manually.

Surge protector. Protect the electronic equipment in your home from the pricy and damaging effects of old wiring and power fluctuations with a simple surge protector.

Rechargeable batteries. The batteries and the recharger are an investment, but you won't have to run out to buy new batteries each time yours run dry.

Digital camera. Skip the cost of film and developing entirely. You're also sure to get a great picture every time because you can take as many shots as you need without worrying about wasted film and developing costs.

Clothesline or clothes rack. Even if you don't hang all your clothing to dry, you can at least prolong the life of delicate items such as bras and sweaters and protect your dryer from hard-to-handle items such as rugs and comforters.

Mesh laundry bags. Protect your clothing investment by guarding delicate items from damage while in the wash. Smaller bags can also be used in the top rack of the dishwasher to hold and protect small items that often get tossed around and lost, or worse, melted at the bottom of the dishwasher such as sippy cup lids, pacifiers, and bottle nipples.

None of these items require a huge financial investment (okay, maybe the larger appliances), but they can help make what you're already paying for stretch further or simply save you from wasting money to begin with.

Pay Less to Uncle Sam

There's no doubt about it: tax time can be stressful. But you can make it less of a burden. A little prep work throughout the year and a little knowledge (or at least knowing where to get information) can go a long way to making tax time easier and even more profitable for you.

Watch Your Withholding

Keep more of your money to meet your needs each month by adjusting your federal tax withholding. Ask to update this information with your employer to ensure that major life changes such as the birth or adoption of a child or the loss of spousal income are reflected in your withheld amount. Use the free calculator available at www.irs.gov to determine how much to have withheld from each paycheck and ensure that you keep as much money as possible on a monthly basis.

By failing to update this information, not only could you be costing yourself money every month, but you're allowing the government to profit from the interest made from *your* money when you could be investing it and profiting instead. You earned it; be sure you keep more of it.

Nickel and Dime Your Deductions

Every little bit counts, especially when you're adding up the total allowable tax deductions you can take.

One of the easiest ways to do this is save your medical and other health-related receipts. True, these expenses are only deductible if they add up to at least 7.5 percent of your *adjusted gross income* (AGI), but there's no way to know if you meet this unless you save each and every receipt over the course of the year. This can be as easy as grabbing a box or an envelope in January and committing to slip every medical receipt inside.

Be sure not to shortchange yourself. It might be obvious to include receipts for doctor visit and

---

def·i·ni·tion

Adjusted gross income, or AGI, is the actual dollar amount used to determine how much tax you owe. AGI is calculated by subtracting allowable adjustments such as IRA contributions, moving expenses, or unreimbursed business expenses from your gross income.

---

prescription co-pays, but don't forget the less-obvious expenses, too. Parking costs when visiting the doctor; dental expenses; and even the cost of eyeglasses, contacts, and their care are deductible. For a complete list of what is an eligible medical and dental expense, visit the IRS website at www.irs.gov and download Publication 502 or call 1-800-829-1040 to request a free copy to be mailed to you.

Apply the same technique to collect charitable contribution receipts throughout the year, too. You can lower your tax liability by deducting monetary giving and donations of goods to any educational, religious, or charitable organization that's approved by the IRS. (To see a complete list, visit the IRS website at www.irs.gov and download Publication 78 or call 1-800-829-1040 to request a free copy.) So request and keep those donation receipts all year long. Generally speaking, as long as the combined total doesn't exceed 50 percent of your AGI, you can deduct them.

Saving at Tax Time

Skip paying a tax professional to do your taxes, and become the expert yourself. The paperwork can give you a migraine, but there are no secrets and there are plenty of resources for free assistance. The IRS website is available 24 hours a day, 7 days a week, or you can even get free help over the phone by calling 1-800-TAX-FORM (1-800-829-3676).

> **Dollar $tretcher**
>
> If you do your own taxes, invest in tax software. Not only is the cost of the software deductible, but it will enable you to take advantage of extra deductions you may not have been aware of, diminishing your tax liability and seriously stretching your money.

If you're not quite ready or willing to go it on your own but still want to save the money of paying someone else, check to see if your local public library offers free tax assistance. Many libraries have set times and days during which volunteers come in to help others prepare their taxes. Be prepared with all your necessary paperwork, records, and receipts, and you could walk out with your taxes done for free.

You can't get better than free, and believe it or not, the IRS allows thousands each year to file their taxes online for completely free. The IRS File Free program does have a maximum income requirement that can change from year to year. For the 2008 tax year, households with AGI of $56,000 or less were able to take advantage of the program. If you're expecting a refund and you're itching for it early, don't pay to file online until you find out if you qualify. You could save yourself a tidy sum of cash. Search www.irs.gov for "free file program" for more information.

Know When to Pay a Little More

You obviously don't want to pay extra for packaging, but in certain situations packaging does count, so it makes sense to be willing to pay a bit more if necessary.

> **Dollar $tretcher**
>
> You can make your own foaming hand soap. Fill any empty foaming soap dispenser with 1 tablespoon liquid hand soap and warm water, leaving about ½ inch space at the top. You might have to pump the dispenser a few times the first time you use it.

For example, vitamin D is often added to milk. However, this nutrient loses its potency rapidly when exposed to sunlight. For that reason, milk packaged in opaque cartons and jugs is a better value. Lotions and facial products dispensed using a tube versus a large tub diminish the chances of bacterial contamination. Products that feature foam dispensing compared to a pump dispenser usually last longer.

Almost any item that performs more than one function is worth its weight in gold, regardless of whether it's an advertised function or not. Baking soda is a phenomenal example of this. Sold primarily as an ingredient for baking, this inexpensive powder works its wonders throughout the house as a mild abrasive cleaner, a deodorizer, and even as a gentle skin exfoliator. Check the box for use ideas, or hop online and do some searching. (Or keep reading for more on the wonders of baking soda.)

What *Not* to Buy

Manufacturers can be masters of disguise when it comes to getting consumers to purchase the exact same product only packaged in different ways. Don't be fooled, and save your money.

If you already have ranch dressing at home, for example, don't go out and buy a separate container of ranch dip; they're the same thing. If you're looking for peanuts to top an ice cream sundae, don't make a special purchase. Use what you already have at home, do your own crushing, and save a tidy sum. Looking for a tool to keep your bags of food closed? Don't spend a premium for clips specifically marketed for this purpose. Head to the stationary aisle or use binder clips or even clothes pins you already have instead.

My favorite example of this packaging ploy is baking soda. In the cleaning aisle, you'll find baking soda carpet deodorizer for a premium price. Head to the baking aisle and you can buy it for less than buck a box. Sure, you do get fragrance added if you opt to buy it in the cleaning aisle, but clean doesn't have a smell. Skip the added smells entirely, and pocket the savings. This also goes for baking soda pet deodorizers. Your pet and your wallet will thank you.

You work hard for your money, so work just as hard to keep more of it where it belongs—with you. Skimp on paying someone else to do for you what you can do for yourself, and you'll save dearly. Just remember, quality of life counts! Becoming a do-it-yourselfer in some areas stretches your dollar and enables you to afford to pay someone else to do the things you'd rather not.

Chapter **5**

Cutting Costs Around the House

In This Chapter

◆ Stretch your home-improvement dollar

◆ Simple changes save on your energy bill

◆ Decorate in style without all the spending

◆ Dollar-stretching bill-paying tips

You have no control over the state of the economy, but you can control what you do within the walls of your home to stretch the dollars you earn. The cost of maintaining and even upgrading your home can be overwhelming. You don't want to feel deprived as costs keep rising, so take steps now to retain and maintain your home, even when the cost of living goes up and up, and make the house you live in one you're proud to call home.

In this chapter, we take a look at ways to keep your house in tip-top shape without draining your checking account, how to improve the energy you use, and even how you can stretch your decorating dollars. And you have to pay for all this, so we also look at the bills you pay, the loans you manage, and smart repayment ideas for both.

Maintaining and Upgrading Your Castle for Less

If you own your own home, it's likely your single greatest investment. If you rent, your housing costs probably comprise your greatest expense. Either way, you're likely shelling out a lot of money on your housing. That doesn't mean, however, that you have to spend big bucks to keep it in prime shape. Quite the contrary; there's never been a better time to build a better castle on a dime.

Super Saver

When purchasing paint, check out the clearance section first. Stores that mix custom colors usually have a special section devoted to selling paint that, for whatever reason, didn't pass final muster with another customer. If you're not super picky, you can often score a super deal on good-quality paint!

The best place to begin is with the smallest changes that reap the biggest result. A can of paint may not cost much, but a splash of new color can breathe new life into a room and can even give the illusion of more space. For a very small financial investment, new pulls on kitchen or bathroom cabinetry can make older cabinets look new again. Spending a few bucks on renting a professional carpet steam cleaner can give the illusion of newer carpet—and can actually extend the life of the carpet.

Free DIY Education and Inspiration

Take advantage of the plethora of training decorating and even construction opportunities in stores, online, and on TV. From the various TV shows devoted to designing on a dime to free DIY workshops at local hardware stores, you can find know-how and inspiration all around you.

Start and keep a file of magazine clippings featuring design ideas you'd like to replicate in your home. Or include photos you snap when you see something your friends or neighbors have done that you like. From landscaping ideas to different color combinations to eclectic furniture arrangements, you can create your own home design consult guide for free and work step-by-step, dollar-by-dollar to get there.

Contractor Do's and Don'ts

Sometimes it just makes good financial sense to employ an expert's skills, such as when remodeling a kitchen or bathroom, for example. Hiring a contractor, however, doesn't have to mean handing over *all* your money.

You may very well be hiring the contractor for their expertise, but that doesn't mean you're hiring them to spend your money. Search for and purchase appliances, fixtures, and necessary supplies yourself so all the contractor has to bill you for is the installation. Just be sure to verify and follow any store return policies, and keep all receipts in case supplies go unused or exchanges need to be made.

Consider hiring a contractor off-season to get a deal. The vast majority of contractors are hired in the summer and spring, when people are eager to make home improvements. If you're open to scheduling contractor time during the slower months of fall and winter, you can open your wallet to better prices.

> **Dollar $tretcher**
>
> Contractors don't always have to cost you money. Trade talents with friends and family to make home improvements without busting your budget. Ask people you know to toot their own horn about hidden talents and skills they may have, and don't forget to share your own to sweeten the deal. If you can strike a mutually beneficial deal, you might not have to pay a dime.

Stretch Smart and Energy Wise

Depending on the season, your power and heating bills are likely some of the larger bills you pay each month—after, perhaps your mortgage, car payment, student loan bill, etc. Still, in the middle of cold-climate winters or tropical-area summers, opening that heating or cooling bill can stop you in your tracks! Fortunately, there are easy ways to make these bills smaller that don't require you live in the dark or turn off the heat or AC.

Easy Energy-Saving Tips

Standard fireplaces may be romantic and appeal to our cave-dweller sense of security; however, they're lousy for actually heating a room, can be dirty, and use a ton of wood. You may want to consider getting a fireplace insert if the lure of fire is too powerful to resist. They're much more efficient in terms of actually heating your home, are *much* cleaner, and use less wood overall.

Let science help stretch your heating dollars. Warm air rises, so during cold months, keep your fireplace flue closed when not in use so warm air doesn't escape and cold air can't enter. Of course, so don't forget to open it back up when you light another fire.

Ceiling fans can also put science to work for your wallet—and not just during the summer months, either. Most fans have a toggle switch that changes the direction the fan blades spin. During winter months, ceiling fans should spin clockwise to help direct warm air down toward the living space to help lower the dependence on heating sources. During the hot summer months, fans should spin counterclockwise to direct hot air up and away.

Stave off the costly habit of continually turning up the thermostat by keeping shades and curtains closed during the day and night throughout the winter months. The extra barrier helps insulate the room against any cold air coming through the windows. It's also much easier and far cheaper to keep a few extra blankets on the bed than to heat the entire room.

Avoid wasting energy by stopping the dryer when the clothing inside is dry—often this is well before the dryer's cycle is finished. Perhaps more important: don't overload your dryer. Less clothing allows for more room to tumble, and that means the dryer can function more efficiently. Whenever possible, dry multiple loads back to back. Heating the air in the dryer is the most energy-consuming part of that appliance. Minimize this cost by utilizing the dryer while it's already hot.

Stretch your energy dollars even further by checking with your power company to see if they offer discounts for usage during nonpeak hours.

Being a good steward of the energy you're purchasing means you'll get more bang for each buck you spend and save more overall.

> **Dollar $tretcher**
>
> After baking, don't waste all that residual oven heat. Leave the oven door open slightly to release the heat into your home. If you have children or pets, be extra careful to keep them clear of the kitchen.

Boost Your Home's Energy Efficiency

Want to make your home more energy-efficient, but don't know where to begin? Enlist free help. Many power companies offer free home *energy audits* to determine how much energy your home uses and how that energy can be used more efficiently. This can translate to a smaller bill for you. Even if your power company doesn't offer such an audit, many websites list specific ways you can conserve energy and thereby, lower your costs. Using energy more efficiently—and simply using less—can mean more green for you and the environment. (See more on green saving ideas in Chapter 13.)

> **def•i•ni•tion**
>
> An **energy audit** is an inspection and analysis of energy use and efficiency, usually in a home, and identifies areas where improvements can be made.

You don't have to have an energy audit to benefit from energy savings. For example, seal any leaks in your windows with caulking or weather stripping, and tape clear plastic film to your metal window frames to immediately save 10 percent or more on your heating bill.

To improve the efficiency of the heat you're already paying for, be sure furniture doesn't block radiators, registers, or baseboard heaters.

Cleaner equipment works more efficiently, so no matter what heating system you use, take care to keep it clean.

You don't just pay to heat the air in your home. Heating your hot water alone can account for 14 to 25 percent of your energy bill. Besides using less hot water, you can also save energy by making sure your hot water tank is adequately insulated with an insulation blanket. Be careful not to cover the tank's thermostat. Speaking of the thermostat, consider setting it at an energy-saving 120°F.

Although more expensive than regular incandescent bulbs, *compact fluorescent lightbulbs* (CFLs) last substantially longer, use about 75 percent less energy, and can save $30 or more in energy costs per bulb over the life of the bulb. Multiply that times the number of bulbs you use throughout your home, and you'll rack up substantial savings.

def•i•ni•tion

Compact fluorescent lightbulbs (CFLs) are safer and cheaper to operate than their incandescent counterparts. They produce about 75 percent less heat, use about 75 percent less energy, and last about 10 times longer.

One caveat to all this energy savings: some electric companies actually charge you *more* money per kilowatt hour if you aren't using what they think you should be using. Before you cut down on your use, call your power company!

Energy-Saving Appliances

It doesn't make good financial or environmental sense to replace a perfectly good appliance if it's still meeting your needs. If it's time to consider such a purchase, however, don't just focus on the impending cost. Instead, think of it as the opportunity to secure bigger savings over the course of the new appliance's life. Over the next few years, the savings you could reap by purchasing a more energy-efficient appliance may very well make up for the cost.

Look for appliances that are labeled energy efficient. Energy Star is a program developed in cooperation with the U.S. Environmental Protection Agency and the U.S. Department of Energy. Energy Star identifies products that utilize less energy and, in turn, can save you money. When shopping for an appliance, look for the Energy Star logo and information, usually posted directly on the appliance itself. The bright yellow tag gives the energy rating for the product; the higher the rating, the more energy you'll save. Energy Star even offers rebates for some qualified purchases. For more information, visit www.energystar.gov.

Decorating on a Dime

You want to be happy with the way things look at home, but you don't want to spend a ton of bucks on changes. Whether you enjoy a shabby, cozy look or you're a decorating diva who likes all things new, your home decorating needn't cost you a pretty penny. All it takes is some creativity, some ingenuity, and a willingness to look at different possibilities in a new light.

Little Changes, Big Results

If you're feeling like it's time for a change, take a stroll through a home improvement store to get your creative juices flowing. Visit the paint section to pick up color chips to help you visualize how adding new splashes of color can help you reinvent a room. Visit the closet-organization section to find storage ideas to re-create at home. Take-home brochures can give you ideas for furniture arrangement you may never have thought of.

Small changes can have a big effect without the accompanying hefty price tag or time investment. Sometimes just a coat of paint can refresh a room and make it look like you redecorated completely. New pulls on cabinets and drawers can update a kitchen. A few new towels and a new shower curtain can breathe new life into a tired bathroom.

Be open to finding new ways of decorating, and you can open your wallet to substantial savings. Who said you have to buy sheets in sets? Purchase sheets and pillowcases separately on clearance or at thrift stores. Keep in mind that sheets do not have to match your comforter! Even your table settings can be mixed up to create an enjoyable eclectic tablescape that stretches your dollars.

 Penny Pitfall

Know when to spend and when to save decorating dollars. Be willing to spend a little extra on items you plan to have around for a while. Show restraint when spending on more trendy items you'll likely switch out for something else in the near future.

When decorating, look for items that can be dressed up—these are often less expensive than the "fancier" items. A simple but sturdy couch can be revved up with a new slipcover. A plain, solid-color comforter can get a punch of style from some colorful pillows. (Make them yourself if you're crafty!) By decorating in inexpensive bits and pieces brought together stylishly, you'll be better able to mix things up more economically when you're ready for a change. After all, changing an accessory here or there is far more stretch-smart than completely redoing a room.

If you're drawn to the worn and mismatched look, don't pay the high price retail stores charge. Head instead to secondhand and thrift stores. You'll reap unbelievable savings and decorate your home with one-of-a-kind accessories. And if you're not thrilled with the color, paint is cheap!

Think Outside the Box

You can get creative with decorating and still keep your budget in check. Allowing tradition to dictate your furniture purchases, for example, can be costly. Don't purchase a huge chest of drawers if you hang the bulk of your clothing in the closet. Like a TV in the bedroom? Don't make the costly assumption that you need to buy a separate TV stand. Make your dresser multi-task as a TV stand. (Just be sure it's strong enough to hold the TV!)

If you need a new bed, purchase a mattress and mattress box that isn't a matched set. If you're willing to purchase a set covered in different fabrics or by different manufacturers, you can save big money. No one will be the wiser with the linens on, but your budget will know the difference. (Some mattress sets are made to work together, though. If this is the case, don't void your warranty by breaking up a set. Savings can still be had. Find out if there's an older model available at a discount.)

 Penny Pitfall

Free isn't always the best way to stretch your dollar. Before you accept any free item, be sure it will really meet your needs. If it isn't, you could not only be stuck with the cost of buying a replacement but also the bill to get rid of it.

Well-placed throw rugs add a punch of color and can help protect greater investments—your carpet and hardwood floors. Colorful placemats can brighten up a bedroom while protecting the tops of dressers and nightstands. Small wall-mounted shelves help decorate plain walls while providing additional storage space.

Instead of replacing something entirely, look for ways to mix the new with the old. Need a new table lamp? Look for a base at a thrift store and top it off with a new shade. Explore your options, and you'll see big savings.

Paying the Bills for Your Castle

Everyone has at least a few monthly bills they have to manage, and you likely feel you don't have much choice when it comes to bills. While you may have limited control over how much is due on your bills, you have complete control over *how* you pay them and, subsequently, how much the act of paying them costs you.

Bills can cost you money in two ways: one is by not paying off the most costly bills on time, and the other is by how you actually pay the bill: by mail, by computer, etc. Let's take a look at your options.

Smart Debt Repayment

Believe it or not, even debt is classified into "good" and "bad." Good debt is credit purchases you need such as a mortgage on a home, a student loan, or a car loan. Bad debt is anything purchased with a loan that isn't truly needed such as almost anything paid for via a credit card.

It's generally best to pay off bad debt first. On the other hand, though, it makes sense to pay off the debt that actually costs you the most first. So pay attention to interest rates. For example, if you have a credit card with a lower, fixed rate compared to the rate on your auto loan, it may very well be worth it to work toward paying down the car loan first even though it's considered good debt.

Some debts might also be tax deductible and cost you less in the long run. Mortgage payments and home equity payments are tax deductible, while car loans are not.

Also look into any programs that might be available if you do have school loans. You might be able to defer or deduct the amount you owe, depending on your overall finances.

Pay Electronically and Save

Another way to pay bills for less is to make changes in the method by which you pay your bills. By paying your bills electronically, for example, through your creditors directly (check out their websites) or through your bank's electronic bill-pay service (again, check online), you can save the cost of a stamp each month and decrease the number of checks you use—and pay for.

When creditors save, you can save, too. It costs businesses money to print and mail out bills, and sending them out via e-mail is much more cost-effective. Find out if your creditors offer paperless statements or bills. Many businesses offer discounts or one-time cash benefits for customers willing to sign up for paperless billing. If you're paying electronically anyway, it makes sense to take advantage of this service, especially if the amount due each month doesn't fluctuate. If you don't see any mention of this service on your bill or the company's website, give your creditors a call.

Dollar $tretcher

Need another reason to go paperless? Think of all those trees spared from being turned into paper! Fewer paper bills and envelopes tossed into the trash mean fewer paper bills and envelopes tossed into landfills, too.

While you're paying your bills online, consider setting up automatic payments that are deducted from your account each month without you having to lift a finger to click a mouse. Many financial institutions now offer this service free of charge to their customers, and it can save you substantial money over time. You'll not only save the cost of postage, as mentioned earlier, but you'll also eliminate the risk of incurring any late fees. With a monthly auto payment, you don't even have to think about it.

With regular on-time payments, you'll help protect and possibly even increase your credit rating, and that can save you a great deal of money the next time you apply for credit.

One word of warning with auto bill payments or deductions: don't allow the convenience to make you complacent about subtracting the amount from your check register. Doing so could cost you a fortune in overdraft fees. Create a master list of all your automatic deductions and divide them according to when you get paid. Each time you enter your paycheck deposit into your register, date and subtract all the ongoing deductions for that time period as well. Then you'll have a more accurate idea of how much money you have left and won't miss any payments.

The Check's *Not* in the Mail

If you'd rather pay your bills the traditional way—writing a check, putting a stamp on the envelope, and walking it to your mailbox—that's okay, too. But remember: there's always the risk of that bill getting lost in the mail, whether it's your fault or the postal service's. When you get word that your payment never made it to your creditor, it's pointless to waste time worrying about how it happened, so instead, focus immediately on what to do to fix the situation fast. Your biggest concern is probably how to avoid incurring any expensive late fees.

There is some good news in this situation: most creditors and businesses offer at least a few days' grace period. The key is to pick up the phone and call customer service pronto. Explain the problem (you got a late payment notice but mailed the check on such-and-such a date) and ask if you may make the payment immediately over the phone using a debit or credit card or even an *electronic check*. Before you get off the phone, verify that your account hasn't been charged any additional fees because you paid over the phone. If so, ask that they be waived. If you're not a perpetual offender, chances are they will be waived. You might still have to pay a late payment fee, though.

Do what you can with your debt management and the method you use to pay your bills so you can be comfortably in the driver's seat, in

def•i•ni•tion

An **electronic check** is a paper check that's had all the information converted and processed electronically. For that reason, there's usually no float time between the time the check is written and the time the amount is deducted from your account.

control of what happens, instead of being a victim of the postal service or other unfortunate circumstances. This might be a good time to look into paying your bills online!

Saving on Monthly Home-Related Bills

We all have different home-related bills to pay each month. Some of you have monthly mortgage payments. Some of you (lucky ducks!) have paid off your mortgage and don't have that monthly bill. Maybe you can't live without high-speed Internet and all the cable TV channels you can flip through. Or maybe you get by fine with free TV and your local library or coffee shop's free Internet offerings. Whatever your situation, you can stretch your dollar in these areas.

Your Mortgage Payment

Anyone who's signed on the dotted line to purchase a home has likely had at least one moment of trepidation when they noted the total amount that will be paid over the course of the loan versus the original purchase amount. Even a great interest rate makes an original price balloon to massive proportions when paid over the course of 15, 20, or 30 years.

You may very well feel like your hands are tied, but rest assured, they're not. Swallow hard and sign, but don't necessarily pay your mortgage note according to the lender's schedule. You do have choices.

For example, you can speed up how quickly you pay off your mortgage and save thousands of dollars in interest fees while seemingly spending the same amount of money each month. Instead of making one monthly payment, your mortgage institution might offer bi-weekly payments. Basically, you pay half of your monthly mortgage every 2 weeks for a total of 26 half payments each year, or 13 full payments. Over the course of a 30-year $250,000 loan with a 7 percent interest rate, that equates to a savings of over $82,000 in interest—and the home would be paid off 6 years ahead of schedule!

Also, keep your eye on mortgage rates until the interest rate dips below the current rate you're paying. If you're paying 7.5 percent on your 30-year mortgage and the interest rates fall to 5.50 percent, call your lender and ask about refinancing your mortgage. Call around to other mortgage companies, too, to find the best deal. You might even be able to switch to a 15-year mortgage at the new rate and keep your monthly payments the same while saving tens of thousands dollars over the years!

Can We Talk?

Phones today can be expensive! Many people have both landline and cell phone and pay large monthly bills on each. Think about cutting back or even cutting out one of these services.

If you use a cell phone and get good reception in your home, cancel your landline and skip the cost of the second phone bill. You likely have many features automatically included in the cost of your cell phone package such as free long distance and voicemail that you'd ordinarily pay extra for on a landline. If the cell phone is a better value, why pay the landline cost?

Cell phones may be convenient and cost-effective, but if you're not careful, the extra fees can add up fast. Be sure your plan fits your usage habits. Do your minutes roll over for future use? If you're constantly paying for overages, would a more expensive plan with more minutes would be a better value?

Pay attention for special offers used to lure in new customers. Even if you're locked into your plan with a contract, you can often negotiate a better deal by agreeing to extend your contract time.

If you only use your cell for emergencies, consider purchasing a cell phone with a prepaid plan and only pay for the minutes you use. The per-minute-fee and access charges may at initial glance seem expensive in comparison, but it's far more stretch-savvy than paying extra for minutes and services you don't use.

If you don't want to give up the second line at home and you already pay for Internet access, consider signing up for *VoIP* service. (For a list of the top 10 VoIP companies, visit www.top10voipproviders.com.) Free long-distance service and voice-mail often come standard.

def•i•ni•tion

VoIP (voice over Internet protocol) service enables you to make phone calls through your regular phone using your Internet access rather than through the phone line.

What's on TV?

Sure, the easiest way to stretch your dollar is to cancel cable TV entirely, but let's face it, that's no fun. Instead of thinking of the cable package as a luxury item, consider ways you can lower the cost and still enjoy the benefits.

> **Dollar $tretcher**
>
> Ask and often you shall receive. It's much cheaper for a company to maintain an existing customer than sign up a new one. When you have the ability to choose a provider for any service, use this to your advantage to secure a better deal.

First, be sure you're not paying for extra channels you don't watch. Find out if a smaller cable package is available or if you can bundle the cost with other services from the same provider for a discount. It may even be possible to negotiate a discount on your bill just for remaining a customer and not switching to a competitor. Take advantage of special offers from competing cable providers, either by making the switch or by using those offers as leverage to get a better deal with your current company.

Your home is your castle, and it should be your sanctuary, too, somewhere you enjoy being but don't have to worry about what you're paying for and what you can or can't afford. The tips, tricks, and techniques in this chapter help you keep it well appointed and maintained without costing a fortune.

Chapter 6

Keep the Car, Cut the Costs

In This Chapter

- ◆ Get more gas for your money
- ◆ How you drive can save you money
- ◆ Take care of your car so it will take care of you
- ◆ Ensure you're getting the best insurance
- ◆ Stretch your car-ownership dollars

Many Americans have their own car, or at least have one car per household, and many of us count on a car to get us where we're going. Maybe the fluctuating gas prices we've seen lately, or that car payment you dread from month to month, has you wondering if selling your car would make financial sense for you.

Before you put a "For Sale" sign in your car's back window, read this chapter. In the following pages, I show you how to easily stretch your car-related dollars—and none of them require that "For Sale" sign.

Cost-Cutting Considerations

These days, gas prices are uncertain, to say the least. They climb to the point of breaking the bank one day and fall to a more manageable level the next. It's hard to tell what price you'll have to pay at the pump each day, which makes budgeting for gas difficult.

If you're in the market to purchase a new car, it makes sense to consider fuel economy. If you already have a car, and you're feeling the pinch from bouncing gas prices and other ownership expenses, don't lose hope. There's much you can do to shed some of the financial burden, no matter what the price of gas. But you can also get more out of the gas you're already using and stretch your dollar at the pump.

> **Dollar $tretcher** _____
>
> Countless online message boards are devoted to every make and model car on the road. Here you'll find the same complaints (and praises) about the car you have and often specific advice and information on how to save money or troubleshoot problems. To find an online community devoted to your car, search for your car's make and model and the words *message board*.

Spending Less at the Pump

Gas stations aren't immune to the pressure of competition. You'll likely find cheaper gas prices in areas with a high concentration of stations. Avoid stations located close to freeway off-ramps where there's no competition to speak of.

Gasoline, like any liquid, expands when it's heated, so purchase gas during the coolest time of the day—usually early morning or during the night. It may not be the most convenient or comfortable time to stand outside and fill your tank, but you'll get more value for each dollar spent. How so? Because when gas is cooler, it's denser, and gas pumps charge by volume, not fuel concentration. By braving the weather, you'll get more gas for your money.

Speaking of filling up, don't overpay at the pump for nothing. Unless your car specifically requires it, avoid paying the high cost of premium fuel. Most modern cars are built to run on the cheap gas. Save your money, select the cheap stuff, and feel no guilt.

As a result of bouncing gas prices, several websites have popped up devoted to finding the best gas prices around. Visit GasBuddy.com and FuelEconomy.gov to scan your neighborhood for the cheapest gas. Don't assume the same place that sold cheap gas yesterday will offer the same price today. Sometimes simply visiting the gas station across the street or a block away can help stretch your gas money even further.

Super Saver

If you use a grocery store loyalty card, find out if it also earns you fuel discounts. Many major stores offer customers per-gallon discounts after a certain amount of points are accrued.

Even the way you pay for your gas can affect your final cost. If you pay with a debit or credit card, some gas stations charge a fee for this. If you visit such a station regularly, a nominal fee here and there can really add up. A gas station that charges a few cents more per gallon, but no service charge for paying with plastic, might actually be the cheaper option. Or simply avoid this decision altogether and pay with cash!

When you're done filling up and you're tightening your gas cap, listen for the click to ensure the seal is tight. Not doing so can allow your gas to evaporate. A gas cap that isn't on tight enough can even account for a "Service Engine Soon" light on your dash, and who wants to pay a service fee to find that out?

Drive Your Way to More Dollars

Saving money on gas doesn't stop at the station. Protect your investment by being proactive about driving in ways that will stretch how much mileage you get from each fill-up. It's easy to maximize your car's mileage by making simple adjustments in your driving habits. Not only will you realize more time passes between fill-ups, but you'll decrease wear and tear on your car as well.

For example, close your windows while driving on the freeway. Keeping your windows open even a crack while traveling at high speeds can create drag and reduce your fuel efficiency by as much as 10 percent. For the same reason, remove bicycle, ski, and luggage racks when they're not in use.

> **Super Saver**
>
> Reset your trip odometer every time you fill up your gas tank. You'll quickly become more aware of what kind of gas mileage your car gets and you can make changes in your driving patterns accordingly. Challenging yourself to lengthen the time and increase the mileage between fill-ups.

Don't be too eager to fill your tank. A lighter car gets better mileage, and all that gas adds weight. Aim to fill up when your tank is only about ¼ full or when you see the prices begin to drop. On the flip side, don't let the needle fall too low. When a car runs on fumes, sediment that usually falls to the bottom of the tank can actually enter the engine and clog and damage parts.

Turn off the AC. While running your car's air conditioner may not be a huge drain on your gas tank, it *does* lower your gas mileage. If you're going to use the air conditioner, turn it off about 5 minutes before you reach your destination to avoid running it the entire time you're in the car. Roll down your windows a crack when you park your car so there's better air circulation while you're gone. And try to park in the shade whenever possible.

Skip the warm-up. Modern cars do not need to warm up before driving, even on cold days. About the same time it would take you to put on your seatbelt and check your mirrors (about 30 seconds) is all the warm-up your car needs. Allowing your car to sit parked and idling is not only a waste of gas, but it pollutes the air unnecessarily and could very well cost you a ticket. In many areas of the country, it's illegal to leave your car idling for a certain length of time.

Speaking of idling, if you're stopped in the car somewhere for more than a minute (like in line at a drive-thru), avoid idling and turn off your car. Idling for more than a minute uses up more gas than restarting the engine. Turning off your car can increase your gas mileage by 19 percent.

Opt for freeway and highway driving over surface streets whenever possible. You'll more likely maintain a constant speed and avoid the stop-and-go of streetlights, which is far more gas-efficient. If you can take advantage of carpool and HOV (high-occupancy vehicle) lanes to avoid any sluggish backup, your gas mileage will be all the better.

If your car is equipped with cruise control, use it. Not only could you be avoiding a costly ticket for speeding, but you'll maintain a constant speed, which will save gas. On average, cruise control can increase your gas mileage between 7 and 14 percent.

Avoid driving on rough roads or through construction zones. You eliminate the cost of idling for long periods of time, and even a slightly longer route can use less gas than idling in construction areas. Driving on unpaved surfaces uses up 30 percent more gas. You'll also save time and possible damage to your car, including dings in the windshield.

Slow down to increase your gas mileage (and maybe ward off a speeding ticket!). Dropping from 65 to 55 miles per hour stretches the value of your gas dollars by adding 2 more miles per gallon. With the high price of gas, that can really add up!

Come to a gradual stop for stop signs and red lights. It's safer, especially in incremental weather, and may give the light enough time to turn green before you come to a complete stop. Thanks to inertia, it takes less fuel to accelerate a car that's already in motion and, therefore, stretches your gas mileage.

Plan your errands and route before you leave home. Staying clear of wrong turns and busy routes can shave time off your commute and stretch the money you spend on gas. Combining as many errands as possible into one outing increases your mileage efficiency by minimizing the number of little outing you need. If you have a GPS (global positioning system), use it. It can help you save gas by finding the most direct route, minimizing wrong turns. Plus, if you know where you're going, you're less likely to speed (are those red and blue flashing lights following you?) because you'll be on the quickest route to begin with.

If you live near a school zone or along a school bus route, do your best to avoid the morning and afternoon pick-up and drop-off times. Getting stuck behind a school bus making stops not only costs you time, but costs gas as well with all the stopping and starting and idling. All that gas guzzling can really add up.

Avoid left turns. Take a dollar-stretching tip from United Parcel Service and the U.S. Postal Service. Strive to find driving routes with the least number of left turns as possible. Often you're forced to let your car sit and idle (wasting gas) while you wait for an opportunity to turn safely. Taking right-handed turns is faster, more gas-efficient, and safer.

Adjust your work schedule. If you work a schedule that places you right in the middle of the commuter crunch, consider asking your employer if you may adjust your work hours to avoid peak travel times. Emphasize it's not about working fewer hours, but adjusting the time you start your work day. Doing so has benefits for your employer, too. You're far less likely to show up to work late if you're not stuck in traffic to begin with.

> **Super Saver**
>
> Is working from home an option for you? Even if you're only able to do a day or two a week, you can limit how often you commute—and how often you pay for gas. You'll stretch your wardrobe budget as well by not having purchase and care for as much work clothing.

It makes good dollar-stretching sense to get the most from your money, including the dollars you spend on gas. Safeguard what you've already paid for by putting these tips to use, and you'll stretch your gas money further while getting point A to point B.

An Ounce of Prevention ...

Prevention is often the best plan of action when it comes to your car. A few dollars spent upfront and a bit of effort before things go wrong are sure to protect your investment—your car—and protect the dollars you could end up paying in repair bills.

Avoid having to pay someone to come and rescue you with a jump if a dead battery ever leaves you stranded. Keep a pair of jumper cables in the trunk of the car—and learn how to use them! It's far easier to get a stranger to agree to give you a jump if you're prepared with the necessary tools.

While you're at it, check the spare tire in your trunk from time to time. Be sure it's still inflated properly and ready to use, and you'll avoid a costly service call. And take inventory of the tools you have at the ready so you don't have to pay someone to come help you. If you're ever caught stranded with a flat, that spare isn't going to do you any good unless you're equipped with the necessary tools to change it.

 Penny Pitfall

Unless you travel extensively or take advantage of the other benefits, avoid the cost of joining an automobile club or association for the roadside assistance benefit. Many auto insurance companies offer similar towing and roadside assistance for a much smaller fee.

Check your tire pressure monthly first thing in the morning with a tire gauge. Not only does this help prevent flat tires, but improves your car's fuel economy as well. For each pound of pressure your tires are underinflated, you stand to lose 6 percent in gas mileage. An added bonus: you'll also lengthen the life of your tires by ensuring equal distribution of wear and tear.

Also, rotate the tires every 6 months or after every 6,000 miles. Not doing so can cut the life of your tires in half.

Heed any warning lights on your dash. It may be very tempting to ignore it, but doing so could end up costing you even more. Better to take your car in to the shop now and have it checked out while it can still get you there than waiting until you need to pay for an expensive tow in addition to the repair work. Staying on top of things and taking care of your car as soon as necessary can help protect the resale value of your car as well.

Protect your dollar by selecting a mechanic as carefully as you would a physician. Do your homework to find a reputable mechanic before you actually need one. Locating a repair shop under the duress of having to fix a car ASAP is not an ideal situation to say the least. Ask around at work, talk to family and friends, and call the Better Business Bureau to find out if the shop is in good standing. You'll have less cause to worry that you're being taken for a ride, so to speak, when you need work done.

Saving in the Shop

Likely the most consistent form of preventative auto maintenance is the oil change. Take steps to verify you're not unnecessarily overpaying for this service, however. Be sure whoever is changing your car's oil is using the correct grade for your particular vehicle. (Find this information in your car's owner's manual.) Oil grade mainly pertains to the viscosity. If the oil being poured into your car's engine doesn't have the correct amount, there will be excessive friction in the engine, leading to poor gas mileage and more wear and tear on the engine.

Don't overdo it, though. Stretch your dollars by knowing what the manufacturer recommends for your car in terms of oil grade and frequency of oil changes, and avoid the cost of recommendations that are more often—and more pricy—than you need. As a very general rule, most cars only need oil changes every 5,000 to 7,500 miles.

Believe it or not, your car's air filter can affect gas mileage. The air filter protects the car's engine from impurities and possible damage, and a dirty filter can mean a contaminated engine that uses more gas. Certainly, do not automatically replace your air filter every time the mechanic suggests to, but do follow manufacturer recommendations and as well as common sense. If it looks dirty, change it. Replacing a dirty filter can increase your gas mileage by 10 percent.

A car with a clean exterior gets better gas mileage. An engine that's taken care of properly can keep running without costly repairs. Keeping the trunk free of unnecessary weight prevents wear and tear on the car and tires and also increases gas mileage. Take care of your car, and it also take care of you—and your pocketbook.

Money-Saving Insurance Insights

Auto insurance can take a costly chunk out of your checkbook. Unfortunately, it can also be difficult to determine the quality of what you're paying for until you ultimately need it. Don't leave anything to chance. As with anything else you spend money on, do your research and comparison-shop to be confident you're getting the absolute best value for your money.

Your driving record isn't the only thing that will determine the cost of your premium. Insurance companies have figured out that, in general, people who are responsible with their money are also responsible drivers, and a higher credit score can often equate to a big savings. Call your insurance company to ask if they offer such a discount. Often, with your permission, they can run a quick credit check over the phone. If your credit passes muster, you'll likely receive a cut in your insurance costs.

Stretch your insurance dollars by ensuring you're not overinsured. Carrying excessive coverage can be costly. Your car is unique in that it's a large purchase that actually *de*preciates in value. Liability insurance is a necessity, but comprehensive, or collision, coverage is not. Over time, the extra money you pay for comprehensive coverage could far exceed the actual value of your car. Call your insurance agent annually to update your comprehensive coverage as your car depreciates or to stop it altogether. Place the money you save into a savings account to help pay for a new car when you need it. You'll not only accrue interest on the extra money you're able to set aside, but you could have a tidy sum of money saved for a down payment later on without out even trying.

Dollar $tretcher

If you've done your homework and shopped around for insurance, it can pay to keep your homeowner's or renter's policy with the same agency as your auto policy. It's easier for you (less contact information to remember), and you'll often profit from a hefty discount as well.

Don't forget to ask for any additional discounts on your premium costs. Assuming the insurance agent automatically offers any such discounts can be a costly mistake. Many companies give you discounts for additional safety features such as airbags, anti-lock brakes, and even daytime running lights. It doesn't have to stop there. Do you have more than one car? Ask for a multiple-car discount. Don't drive much to begin with? Ask for a low-mileage discount. Insuring someone under 18? If he or she is a good student, be sure to ask for a good student discount. Be friendly and be polite, but *do* ask for discounts.

Even More Car-Related Savings

If you have a car loan, you're already used to making the payment each month. When it's all paid off, continuing making the payment—to your savings account. You won't feel the crunch of adding the extra money to savings, but when you need to make your next car purchase, you'll definitely appreciate having the extra money already set aside. Money talks, but cash screams, and the more cash you have at your disposal at the time of purchase, the more likely you are to get a better price.

This cash reserve can also come in handy when unexpected, costly repairs pop up. Having the money already available makes it easier to attend to the repairs immediately rather than putting it off. While it may be tempting to procrastinate repair work until the money is available, doing so can sometimes cause more damage and end up costing you even more money later on.

With a little planning and a bit of knowledge, it can be easy to get more out of your car for less. So stay on the road and keep your car—just spend less money doing it.

Chapter 7

Health Care Without the Hefty Cost

In This Chapter

◆ Health products: what to buy, what to avoid

◆ What if you're uninsured?

◆ Health insurance extras

◆ Medication for less

◆ Home remedies

Staying healthy is one of our primary concerns. But sometimes, when even if you're lucky enough to have health insurance, the coverage just isn't enough and you have to pay more out-of-pocket than you'd like. In fact, the very cost of health insurance can make you sick to your stomach!

Take heart, though. You can minimize your health-care expenses while securing the best care possible.

Practice Prevention, Save $$$

It's always more cost-effective to prevent a problem than to try to fix it later, especially when it comes to your health. Aside from the obvious—maintaining healthy eating habits and an active lifestyle—there are other, less obvious ways to cut your health-care costs.

 Super Saver

Stave off illness any time of the year and especially during cold and flu season by simply practicing good hygiene. Cover your mouth when you sneeze or cough. Wash your hands. Use hand sanitizer. It's really that simple!

You probably don't think about saving money by staying healthy, but this is one of the easiest ways to keep more money in your pocket. Instead of spending money on medicines when you're sick, you can put it toward something that will increase your standard of living and make you happier.

Products Worth Spending Money On

Some products truly are worth their weight in gold when it comes to your health. They don't necessarily cost much either. Alcohol-based hand sanitizer is one example. Use it when you're out and about and can't wash your hands. This inexpensive product can make a world of difference in your health—and your pocketbook when you don't have to shell out for cold medicines and doctor's visits.

Lip balm is another good product to have on hand. Skip the expensive facial tissue with lotion and stretch your dollar by protecting and moisturizing your sore nose with unflavored lip balm. Relief is immediate, and the balm helps protect the irritated skin from the elements, too. (Just be sure that each family member has his or her own balm for nose-use-only!)

Products to Skip

Good intentions may have you reaching for your wallet to purchase some health-related items, but don't be so fast to whip out your cash. You can skip some purchases and pocket the savings without detriment to your health.

If you eat well-rounded meals that meet your nutritional needs, don't waste your money on vitamins. If your body doesn't need them, they simply leave your body when you urinate anyway. Stop flushing money down the toilet, literally, and stop wasting your money on nutritional supplements.

As with any other purchase, name-brand products aren't necessarily better. In fact, the contrary can often be true. Name-brand drugs often come in flashy packaging with extra ingredients that jack up the price. Read the labels, and you'll likely find you can take advantage of generic medications that come with a smaller price tag as well as fewer ingredients you really don't need anyway.

Penny Pitfall

Read the labels on over-the-counter medications carefully for potency and dosage instructions. Generic drugs aren't truly cheaper if you have to take more of them to get the same effect.

Help for the Uninsured and Underinsured

It's a sad reality that not all employers provide health-care benefits to their employees. Even if an employer covers the cost of providing benefits for the employee, there are times when that employee has a family of his or her own to provide benefits for. Whether this is the case for you or you simply don't have access to health care to begin with, there are ways to get good health care without breaking the bank.

First and foremost, don't go it alone if you don't have to. Many states offer free or low-cost health-care programs for children under 18, and some even offer the same insurance benefits to adults. To find out more, contact your state's department of social and health services.

Paying for Medical and Dental Care

Just as you can count on the sun rising tomorrow, you can bet that eventually life will throw your bottom dollar a curve ball. Chances are, it will be of a health-related variety.

It would be impossible to plan for every unexpected expense, but you can be proactive so you're not caught off guard when something does come up. If you're ever caught in need of medical or dental care and you don't have insurance (or need a service that's not covered by your policy), ask for a *cash discount* or about any possible payment plans available to you.

def•i•ni•tion

A **cash discount** is a price reduction based solely on a customer paying with cash. Cash discounts aren't reserved only for car or other big-ticket-item purchases. If you have cash ready to pay for any expense, you're more likely to get a lower price, so don't forget to ask.

In fact, many doctors and dentists offices offer payment plans without charging any interest, especially if you're a long-standing patient. Establishing a payment plan with the office or provider directly is far and away preferential to paying with a credit card. You'll likely avoid any additional fees, and you'll still have the flexibility of paying over time.

Take advantage of free community services. Chances are your tax dollars are paying for it anyway. Stop in at a local fire station to have your blood pressure checked properly. Visit the public health department for free or low-cost vaccinations. If your health ever truly suffers, visit an emergency room. Many hospitals have a standing policy not to turn away patients simply due to an inability to pay. To be sure you're not clobbered with a big bill later on, however, make a quick call to the hospital in advance to inquire about their policies regarding inability to pay. Even if they're unable or unwilling to help, they'll most likely be able to direct you to other resources that can.

Getting Help with Prescriptions

A lack of health insurance doesn't have to mean an inability to save on prescription medications. Several programs are available to help the uninsured get access to prescription drugs at reasonable rates. Some of these programs are absolutely free.

Together Rx Access is a prescription discount program that was created by and continues to be sponsored by leading pharmaceutical companies. It was designed to make prescriptions more accessible to everyone, including the uninsured. This program is limited to citizens of the United States and Puerto Rico and those who do not otherwise have prescription drug coverage. Together Rx Access is completely free, offers savings of between 25 and 40 percent off name-brand drugs, and has no maximum usage limits. For more information, call 1-800-444-4106 or visit www.togetherrxaccess.com.

Super Saver

If you have a membership with AAA, you can enroll in its free prescription drug savings program. The program is accepted at 9 out of 10 pharmacies and can be used for all family members, even pets. On average, members save 24 percent off each prescription purchase. Visit www.aaa.com or call 1-800-562-2582 for more information.

True Care Advantage is a similar program. It's also completely free, can be used to get discounted prescriptions for everyone in the family, and has no age or income requirements. An additional benefit of this program is its mail-order prescription program. It enables even the uninsured to get maintenance medications in bulk at a discounted rate. For more information, call 1-800-747-6190 or visit www.truerxdiscount.com.

Access2wellness is a large, umbrella program that offers several tiers of assistance to the uninsured or underinsured. Sponsored by Johnson & Johnson Healthcare Systems, Inc., access2wellness is one of the broadest assistance programs offering discounts on more than 1,000 different medications. Some of the programs do have financial and age requirements, but some do not. To find out if you qualify or to get more information, call 1-866-317-2775 or visit www.access2wellness.com.

Dollar $tretcher

If you don't have insurance or can't afford your prescriptions, call the pharmaceutical company directly, or call the Partnership for Prescription Assistance Program at 1-888-4PPA-NOW (1-888-477-2669) or visit www.pparx.org. Many major companies now have programs to help patients get their medications for free or nearly so.

If you do have prescription coverage and take an over-the-counter (OTC) drug regularly, ask your doctor if there's a prescription generic available. Don't make the costly assumption that the OTC version is less expensive than any co-pay you may have to shell out. You may be able to save a tidy sum of money by purchasing a multiple-month supply at once through the pharmacy compared to buying it off a drug-store shelf. (For more on how to stretch your prescription dollars, see the "Saving on Medications" section later in this chapter.)

Cashing In on Health Insurance Benefits

If you're fortunate enough to have health insurance, take advantage of every opportunity to squeeze the maximum value from it. Whether you're paying for it or your employer is, that little plastic card is a veri-table wealth of resources and savings.

To determine what exactly your plan offers, ask your employer for a plan handbook, or call the insurance company directly to speak to a plan specialist. There may very well be some obscure benefit that didn't seem worth mentioning to anyone else that could benefit you directly in a very real way.

For example, my insurance company doesn't cover any form of birth-preparedness classes. It wasn't until I called to complain about this that I was told of an additional benefit offered: weekly calls from a registered nurse to answer questions and track the progress of my preg-nancy, free books of my choice, *and* a free retail store gift card.

Managing Your Money with FSAs

All medical expenses are tax deductible, not just premium amounts paid for health insurance. In an effort to help employees keep more of their monthly paychecks, some employers offer optional *flexible spending accounts* (FSAs) as an additional benefit.

def•i•ni•tion
A flexible spending account (FSA) is an account into which employees can deposit pretax money from their paychecks. From this account, only qualified health expenses can be paid. The key advantage of a FSA is its ability to lower your tax liability.

If you or your spouse's employer offers a FSA, consider taking advantage of it. After signing up, you'll need to determine how much money to set aside in it. You'll then be issued a special debit card that accesses the funds to pay for any health-related expenses such as doctor visit co-pays, prescription purchases, or even OTC medications.

Taking advantage of a FSA can really stretch your dollar because the funds are taken out of your paycheck pretax and, therefore, lower your tax liability. On the other hand, some FSA plans are "use it or lose it," and if you don't use up the money in the account by the end of a given period, you lose it.

FSAs can be great to stretch the health-care dollars you're going to spend, but don't get caught in the trap of *not* using them. If you're not a good planner, this probably isn't a good option for you.

Making the Most of Insurance "Extras"

Many insurance companies are catching on to the fact that if they help educate their policyholders and aid them in caring for themselves in appropriate ways, everyone wins. Doctors visits, laboratory fees, and prescription drug expenses cost everyone money—you and your insurance company.

These days, insurance company websites are no longer just an advertisement of services and contact information. They're now powerhouses of free information provided to help individuals care for themselves better. The next time you have a health-related question or concern, log on to your insurance company's website to see what information you can find. It could very well save you the cost of a doctor's visit, not to mention you could get the information and/or relief you need even faster. (Of course, if you have a serious medical concern, go to the doctor!)

If your health insurance offers a 24/7 nurse line to help address health concerns, take advantage of it. It's a free education and medical consultation, and you don't even have to wait until office hours. You're paying for this service through your insurance premiums, so use it. Sometimes we spend our own valuable time and resources researching medical items that a nurse could answer promptly. Remember, time is money!

Better to call the nurse than spend your own valuable time that might better spent elsewhere.

Super Saver

If you're fortunate enough to have double medical coverage through your employer and your spouse's, take full advantage of it. By submitting both insurance cards when purchasing prescriptions, visiting the doctor, or undergoing medical treatments, you'll likely save a tidy sum in co-pay costs.

Saving on Medications

Ouch! The price of prescriptions can almost be as painful as skipping them entirely. Even if you have prescription benefits, accompanying co-pays can add up quickly. Get the prescriptions you need and keep the costs at a minimum by trying a variety of alternative tactics.

If the cost of a prescription drug is prohibitive, ask your doctor if there's an OTC equivalent you can try first. You may very well be able to take an OTC drug at a dosage other than the labeled directions state to achieve the same results as a prescription drug—for substantially less.

OTC drugs, while they don't require a prescription, are just as potent and can be just as dangerous, *so never self-medicate.*

Behind the Pharmacy Counter

Not all OTC drugs are out and readily available on store shelves. Limiting yourself to only this selection greatly decreases your options as well as your possible savings.

Take iron supplements, for example. You can make a selection based on what you find on your own in the aisle, or you can ask at the pharmacy counter. They'll likely have a generic bottle of the same potency for pennies on the dollar compared to what you would have paid from the previous selection. It's a misconception that only prescription drugs are behind the pharmacy counter.

Take advantage of your store's pharmacist as well. She is a wealth of free information and can help you make safer, more effective, and stretch-savvy medication choices. She can also help you get the greatest efficacy from your medication purchases by filling you in on what you need to know, including OTC drugs. You won't know if you don't ask, and your store employs them as a free service to you, so use it.

Getting Your Rx for Less

If the cost of your medications are leaving you feel ill, you can help stretch your prescription dollars. No, I'm not talking about skipping doses!

If you take maintenance medications long term, check out the drug manufacturer's website for coupons. Pharmaceutical companies are keenly aware of the fact that consumers have choices when it comes to the medications they take. To encourage business, they often provide printable coupons on their websites as well as loyalty programs for ongoing savings.

 Super Saver

Don't be shy about asking your doctor for samples of prescriptions you take. He gets them for free from pharmaceutical representatives and likely gives them to patients who need the financial assistance. Stretch your dollar by asking for them.

Don't make the costly assumption that all these savings opportunities will be advertised, either. Pharmaceutical companies, like every other company, are out to make a profit. Seek out the savings on their website, and often you shall find.

Another easy way to stretch your Rx dollars is to purchase via a prescription mail service or a mail-order pharmacy. Not only will you save money, but you'll save monthly trips to the pharmacy as well. You may have to purchase several months' worth of the medication at a time, but many insurance companies offer additional discounts to offset this expense, either by offering bulk discounts or a 3-month supply for the price of 2 months.

Tried-and-True Home Remedies

For all the conveniences and advances our modern society has afforded us, it seems we've given up something of great importance and value—self-reliance. A well-stocked home first-aid kit and a few other small essentials can make the difference between immediate relief and waiting until office hours. Not to mention, the difference in cost.

First, Do No Harm

Before we get to any home remedies, a word of caution: just because something can be purchased over-the-counter or is readily available at home does not mean that it's any less potent or needn't be used with the same amount of care. Quite the contrary. Many home remedies are still around because they do work and work well. Call a pharmacist, take advantage of a nurse hotline, or at the very least consult a medical website such as www.webmd.com for more information before jumping right in.

The greatest dollar-stretching tip out there is to use common sense. If you're suffering from an ailment or illness and it's simply not getting better, make an appointment with a medical professional. When you do, though, don't miss an opportunity to educate yourself. Be sure to ask about anything you might be able to do in the future at home to bring relief.

Stocking Your Home-Remedies Kit

Now, back to that kit! Use the following list as a starting point for items that can bring relief and remedy for pennies on the dollar:

- *Baking soda.* Mix with water to form a paste for soothing insect bites, rashes, and other skin irritations.

 Penny Pitfall

Never give honey to children under the age of 1 due to a risk of botulism.

- *Honey.* A little honey has been proven to soothe and improve coughing better than the over-the-counter drug dextromethorphan or no treatment at all.

◆ *A bag of frozen peas.* Ready at all times, it creates an instant, mold-able ice pack and can be used again and again. (Just don't eat the peas after using it as an ice pack!)

◆ *Epsom salt.* Add to a warm bath to relieve itchy skin or soothe aching muscles. It can also help alleviate athlete's foot and other skin ailments.

◆ *Saline nose drops or spray.* These bring safe, quick relief to irritated sinuses and allergy symptoms by cleaning out nasal passages and thinning mucus, making it easier to breathe.

◆ *Acetaminophen or ibuprofen.* These two standbys are tried and true for a reason: they work. Save your money by not buying OTC drugs that contain additional medications you may not need. Acetaminophen and ibuprofen lower fevers and help alleviate all kinds of pain, from headaches to muscle pain to sinus discomfort.

These are just a few examples of the kinds of products to keep on hand for dollar-stretching home health care. Compound your savings even more by purchasing store-brand or generic options when available.

Finding Home Health-Care Help

You don't have to be a chemist to concoct great homemade solutions to various health-care concerns. From liniment to mouthwash to even anti-dandruff lotions, recipes abound, enabling you to get the results you need at the price you want. Check out www.MyHomeRemedies. com or www.GrannyMed.com to get started.

Another easy way to get started is to simply start looking at the ingredients of products you already purchase. From there, you likely can make better spending decisions that will enable you to stretch your dollars while achieving the same results. Skip the excessive cost of stress-relieving aromatherapy sprays, and make

 Penny Pitfall

Always seek medical advice about the safety of any medication or home remedy. You don't always know how something will affect your specific health concerns and needs.

your own with a few drops of essential oils (found in markets featuring a natural foods section) mixed with water and added to a spray bottle. Forgo the expensive antiseptic wound wash and opt for the cheaper, but just as effective, hydrogen peroxide. Don't pay a premium for specially packaged hemorrhoid pads when you can get the same results with witch hazel and toilet paper or a cotton ball at home.

Health-care costs are expensive, there's no way around it. Continued good health, though, is priceless. Ease the cost by wisely managing the different health resources available to you. Take advantage of what you can, where you can, whenever you can, and see your health-care dollar really stretch, and you'll get more health care for your money. Maybe you can stretch it all the way to the best kind of preventative care available: a nice relaxing vacation!

Chapter 8

Only *Look* Like a Million Bucks

In This Chapter

- ◆ Get more for your clothes-buying cash
- ◆ Cost-effective cosmetics and skin care
- ◆ Know when to skimp and when to splurge
- ◆ Stretch your hair-care dollars

Hardly a day goes by that I don't hear someone complain about the cost of looking good, whether it's clothes, personal care products, or makeup. Stop feeling frustrated!

Arm yourself to shop savvy, learn to protect and prolong the items you buy, and improve the quality of your life—and maybe your looks—by getting more by spending less.

Outfitting Yourself for Less

The cost of the shirt on your back shouldn't eat a hole in your pocket. While prices on everything, including clothing, continue to climb, you can still stretch your wardrobe dollar. Knowing where to go, what to look for, and what to do helps keep you and your family well dressed and your wallet full.

You Get What You Pay For

There's more than a grain of truth in that old saying. Clothes that feature reinforced seams, wrinkle- and stain-release fabrics, and extras such as lined interiors or reversibility cost more for a reason—they stay looking good longer. Be willing to pay a bit more for clothing items that will wear well for a long period of time. Everyday shoes, suits, or overcoats you want to last are worth the extra buck for longevity.

When it comes to purchasing trendy items that have a relatively short fashion shelf life, know when to limit what you spend appropriately or, at the very least, know when and where you can get it cheap such as retail discounter. For instance, every summer I buy new white T-shirts because last year's just don't look as bright. For these, because I replace them every year, I might buy the most inexpensive shirts I can find. (If you don't want to buy new ones every year, you can buy better-quality Ts and bleach them when they start to get dull.)

Wardrobe Shopping Do's and Don'ts

To fill your closet with great clothes and your wallet with even bigger savings, shop off-season. Take stock of what needs replacing for next year's seasonal wardrobe, and buy it at the end of the season when you can snag it on clearance and pack away for later. You'll not only save money by purchasing it discounted, but you'll ready to go with a great new wardrobe come next year.

Unless you're window shopping for style ideas, don't shop at the mall to stretch your clothing dollar. Malls are filled with small boutiques and large department stores, both of which can demand high prices. Stretch your dollar by shopping elsewhere.

To protect your clothing investments, do keep stain remover near the laundry hamper where you remove your clothes. You'll be more likely to stop stains from setting in if you pretreat before you wash, and your clothing will last longer.

Do check the care instructions before you buy. Avoid "dry clean only" garments. Natural fibers are usually easier to care for at home and withstand wear longer. They may require more ironing, but they'll last longer. Synthetics such as polyester are usually made from petrochemicals. That means anything oil or grease based that happens to touch them becomes part of the fabric. When it does, there's virtually nothing you can do to remove the stain.

Do ask employees at your favorite store which day of the week clothing is generally discounted. By knowing in advance, you can first pick at a great price.

Don't narrow your options to only the size you *think* you wear. One brand's medium may very well be another brand's large. Look for what you like, look for a great deal, and always try on everything for size. You may very well be overlooking phenomenal values just because you're taking clothing size for granted. Clothing manufacturers are commonly using *vanity sizing* these days to appeal to shoppers' self-esteems. They're banking on consumers purchasing a particular brand if they can say they wear a size 2 in it rather than a size 8 in another brand.

def•i•ni•tion

> Vanity sizing refers to clothing manufacturers' practice of increasing clothing sizes and keeping the tag's size number the same.

Be open to new shopping experiences and venues to realize greater savings and value. Trunk shows, for example, can be a great way to snag designer fashion at a fraction of the price. As the name implies, this shopping experience entails the designer hauling in their wares by the trunk full to show off and hopefully sell. As a result, special pricing often abounds.

Smaller boutiques can also offer different ways to save. They may very well not have the buying power as bigger retailers do, but smart boutique owners often run special sales just for loyal customers in an effort encourage repeat business.

Do check out thrift stores, and you'll see that these stores sell more than just used clothing. Excess stock from retail stores is often donated to secondhand stores, where it's sold for a fraction of the cost. This is especially true at the end of every season. When you're done checking the clearance racks in retail stores, head to your local thrift store.

While you're at the thrift store, see if you can spot any top-quality designer clothing. These designer gems will probably only have been worn a time or two and then discarded by someone with a lot more disposable income to spend on clothes. You can look like a million bucks and spend just a handful!

When shopping for preowned clothing, be willing to take a calculated risk. Know what can be fixed and what can't. Time is money, and many people would rather get rid of their clothing than fix minor imperfections. If a shirt is missing a button, look for an extra button sewn on an inside seam to replace it, or consider replacing all the buttons entirely. If the bottom of a skirt or a pair of pants shows some wear, trim and hem them a bit shorter. If there's a stain, consider whether or not you can remove it with the help of an oxygen-powered laundry product.

Accessories such as shoes, jewelry, handbags, and even eyeglasses can also be had for a song if you're willing to be a bit adventurous about acquiring them. Test drive in traditional brick-and-mortar stores to determine exactly what you want, then hop online to find a better price. Try on shoes and walk around in the store to determine the exact size, brand, and style you want. Visit a department store to check out the size and pockets in various handbags to determine the best fit for your needs. Check out a high-end jewelry store to figure out the right size of earrings for your frame in person. Sure, shopping online can help you save a bundle, but admittedly it can be difficult to ensure you're going to get exactly what you want. Increase your chances of online shopping success by doing a bit of hands-on, covert research in local shops first.

When shopping for new eyeglass frames, consider trying on and selecting a specific frame in the store, making a note of the exact model number and then tracking them down on eBay or even from an online optical shop to realize great savings. Some optical shops may charge an additional fee for putting new lenses in existing frames (or frames you've purchased elsewhere), but such a fee is usually nominal and even with the added expense can often be much less expensive.

Clothing for Kids

I talk more about stretching your dollars where your kids are concerned in Chapter 9, but I will mention kid's clothes here because chances are, you can use all the dollar-stretching tips you can get. I probably don't have to tell you about kids' clothes and the outrageous prices they command. But I can tell you how you can get more for your dollars.

Hand-me-downs are a great way to get gently used clothing for next to nothing, but your kiddo might feel weird wearing the clothes of someone he sees often, especially if they're friends. Protect your stretching efforts by making hand-me-downs less of a stigma. Instead of getting clothes from his friends who may later on recognize their old clothing, try setting up a trade or purchase of preowned clothing via Craigslist. Your checkbook *and* your child will be happier!

Shirts and underwear featuring the latest cartoon characters can cost a tiny fortune. Keep your money, and let your child be the clothing artist. Supply solid, light-colored basics and fabric crayons or markers, and let your Picasso create her own wearable masterpieces. Anything you can print from your computer can also be transferred to clothing using heat-transfer paper found at any office supply store. (Just be sure you can legally copy and reproduce the image.)

Invest in a few large plastic tubs with lids and scour garage sales, thrift stores, and clearance racks for great deals on clothes in your children's future sizes. Launder and simply tuck away the clothing so you can "go shopping" at home later. Even if you have an older child who is a slave to fashion, you can still look for certain items at a discount and stash them away until later. Just be sure to get your teen on board by sharing that if you're able to purchase some items at a lower price now, there will be more money available later for more stylish, trendy purchases.

Avoid the temptation to fill a closet with cute clothing your child may only wear once or twice. Children sprout up like weeds so quickly that they may only get a few wears out of each item. If you absolutely can't resist, take advantage of consignment shops and thrift stores filled to the brim with barely worn baby and toddler clothing. Often you can find brand-new clothing with the tags still attached purchased with good intentions, only to have a child grow too quickly.

Penny Pitfall _____

It may be tempting to purchase children's clothing a size or two ahead and just roll up pant legs and sleeves, but don't compromise price for safety. Clothing that's too large for a child can be a hazard. Shirts that drape too much, sleeves that are too loose, and pant legs that can unroll past the back of shoes can cause all kinds of accidents.

Kids will be kids. There will be spills. There will be grass stains. There will be pulled buttons. To stretch your dollar, know and prepare for how your child may prematurely wear out her clothing. A quick spray of Scotchguard on the front of a shirt can save it from set-in stains. Purchasing dark-colored pants is a preemptive strike against knees that are forever grass-stain green. A needle and thread to tighten buttons before they're even loose can prevent one from becoming MIA later. Stretch your dollar by preventing the need to not spend more.

Beauty for Fewer Bucks

Oftentimes the better we look, the better we feel. Unfortunately, it's very easy to go overboard in your search for million-dollar looks and buy, buy, buy. The trick is to spend fewer beauty bucks but get more value for what you spend.

Know Where to Shop

Walk right past the cosmetic boutiques and costly cosmetic counters at department stores, and opt instead for purchasing in bulk via mail order, through home-shopping networks, or through discount websites. As long as products are not opened prior to purchase, it doesn't matter how you obtain your cosmetic supplies, only that you're getting the best possible value for the money you spend. Do take special care to not overpurchase, though. If you can't use up a cosmetic prior to the expiration date, it's no savings at all.

Beauty supply stores can be a great resource for high-quality, inexpensive beauty supplies, and not all of them require you to have a cosmetologist's license to shop there. Everything from salon-quality shampoos; hair colorant; brushes; and electronic equipment such as clippers, hair dryers, and curling irons can be found. Some even sell discounted cosmetics and facial- and nail-care products as well.

Get a free insurance policy of sorts with all your cosmetic purchases by shopping at stores that allow you to exchange or return cosmetics if they're the wrong color. Even if a tester was provided, a store's fluorescent lights might make it tough to tell what a color will really look like on you. By shopping at stores that allow returns, you'll never be stuck with a full pretty-in-the-tube lipstick you can't use or a blush that only looks good in the package. Then you'll have more to spend on higher-end products or you can get more variety with the savings you'll see, thanks to no more wasted products!

Dollar $tretcher

Enjoy painting your nails, but hate paying the price for those tiny little bottles every few months? Store nail polish in the refrigerator, and it'll last longer. (*Psst!* Perfume also lasts longer if stored in the fridge.)

Beauty-Boosting, Money-Saving Tips

If you'd like a makeover, an education on proper cosmetic application, and maybe even a few samples, schedule a consultation at the cosmetic counter of any major retail store. True, the entire purpose is to get you to spend money on their products, but it's also a great opportunity to try new, high-quality products for free while having trained personnel select colors that work best on you. It can also be a great free activity for friends to do together.

Home shopping networks have countless beauty products for sale, and most feature lengthy on-air demonstrations on how to use the products. Flip on the tube and sit back to get a free education on everything from how to shape your eyebrows to how to experiment with eye shadows. The trick is to take what you want from the programming (the tips and tricks) and leave what you don't (the products themselves). Hide your credit cards to stop yourself from impulse buying!

Stroll through trendy department stores to window shop for makeup, wardrobe, and hairstyle ideas. These stores are often ahead of the game as far as predicting what the next hot looks will be, giving you plenty of time to score the look for a cheaper price somewhere else.

Dollar $tretcher _____

Hair color treatments can be costly. Don't wash the hair color—and your money—down the drain by overwashing your colored hair. Applying hair-care products that contain UV blockers can also lengthen the life of your color. To lengthen the time between color treatments, and the overall value of what you've already spent, get root-only treatments when you can.

When to Skimp

Protect your bottom line by not paying for things you don't need. You purchase perfume and body spray for their scent; you don't purchase your eye shadow or blush for that reason. Be wary of products that use additional, unnecessary ingredients as fillers because you'll usually end up paying for it and getting little in return.

Be willing to skimp on product packaging and extras such as disposable applicators, and spend more money where it really counts—on the product itself. High-end, highly concentrated eye shadows and blushes, for example, often come with very little packaging and rarely come with a complimentary applicator. Make the one-time investment in a set of good-quality cosmetic brushes, and apply the subsequent savings to the cost of the cosmetics themselves.

When to Splurge

When it comes to cosmetics, price can be an indicator of value. A higher-end product may command a more expensive price, but it likely contains better ingredients and may feature more concentrated pigment as well as longer staying power, which means you'll need to use less of the product to achieve the desired result.

Be smart! On the packaging of any product, cosmetics and beauty supplies included, ingredients are listed in order of content. The higher on the list the ingredient is, the more the product contains. For that reason, it's more cost-effective to splurge on more-expensive products that list a desired active ingredient higher on the list than less-expensive alternatives that may list the same ingredient near the bottom. You'll likely achieve a better result by using less of the product and stretch your supply as well as your dollar.

Penny Pitfall

The safety and effectiveness of cosmetics and skin-care products do not have to be proven to be used in advertising. Because the Food and Drug Administration does not view them as drugs, there's also no true distinction between active and inactive ingredients. Protect your money by searching the ingredient list for specific products known to have beneficial or harmful effects, and purchase accordingly.

Skin-Care Savers

Moisturizers are a phenomenal value when it comes to skin care. They add to overall skin comfort and texture of your skin and enable you to get greater results with less makeup. Moisturizer prices can range from cheap to steep. Stretch your dollar by not paying for something you don't need. For example, it's important to use a moisturizer that contains a sunscreen for daywear, but use a less-expensive moisturizer without it at night.

Dollar $tretcher

Skip spending money on store-bought skin exfoliators and head to your pantry instead. No measuring needed, simply mix ingredients to your desired consistency; usually a 1:1 ratio works best. For a mild exfoliator, mix warm water with baking soda or ground oats until a soft paste forms and apply directly to the skin. For a more luxious, moisturizing exfoliator, slowly mix granulated sugar with olive oil to form a paste.

Hair-Care Help

There are countless ways to trim the cost of keeping up your tresses. An easy way to start is by simply using less product. You're likely using much more shampoo than you need to, for example. Use less, and focus on your scalp area only. While you rinse, work the remaining suds into the ends of your hair to clean the rest. You'll not only make your shampoo supply last longer, but you won't strip your hair of its natural moisture.

Speaking of moisture, relying on store-purchased leave-in moisturizing products and treatments can drain your beauty dollars dry. Instead, head to the kitchen. Wet your hair with warm water, massage a few tablespoons olive oil into your hair, and cover with a plastic bag. Let this set for at least 30 minutes and then shampoo as usual. Olive oil is a natural moisturizer and improves hair strength and elasticity.

And it doesn't make good dollar-stretching sense to pay for conditioner and then rinse it out, only to purchase yet another conditioner to leave in. For an inexpensive yet effective leave-in conditioner, mix 1 part conditioner to 4 parts water, pour into a spray bottle, and shake before each use. Apply it to wet hair to help with styling or to dry hair to help tame frizzy and flyaway hair.

When it comes to cutting your tresses, it makes good sense to purposefully select a style that will look good between haircuts, even as it grows out. It's convenient, and it's also pocketbook-savvy, too.

> **Dollar $tretcher**
>
> Beauty schools can be a great place to treat yourself to a phenomenal cut at a cheap price. Worried? Don't be. All students must be supervised by a licensed professional.

If a few guys live in your household, consider picking up a pair of professional hair clippers and becoming an in-house barber. A complete set of clippers and guides will more than pay for itself with only one cut. Many even come with free how-to guides to teach you not only how to use the clippers, but how to achieve specific cuts as well.

It's simple: when you look better, you feel better. And as the smart dollar stretcher knows, you don't have to spend a fortune to look good; just look like you did!

Chapter 9

Financing Child- and Pet-Care Costs

In This Chapter

- ◆ Keeping your kids and your wallet happy
- ◆ Saving money on car seats without sacrificing safety
- ◆ Getting the most for your pet-care dollars
- ◆ New ways to use everyday items for your pets

Few things in life are as rewarding as raising children and caring for pets. Few things are as expensive, too! Caring for these lovable beings need not break your bank, though. From preemptive planning to innovative solutions, there are countless ways to make sharing a household with kiddos and furry critters easier to bear financially. By stretching your imagination and your dollars, your children can leave you with an empty nest, not an empty wallet, and your pets needn't drain your budget dry. (For more on outfitting your children for less, see Chapter 8.)

Dollar-Stretching Toy Tips

I don't know about you, but I don't remember all my toys making loud noises and flashing bright lights. The cost of batteries alone to keep today's toys running can burn a hole in a budget. Do your budget and your kids a favor, and facilitate a healthy imagination by limiting such glaring toys. Emphasize quality over quantity, and you'll immediately cut toy costs and foster your children's creativity.

Learn to look at items around the house differently to stretch the creative play with little or no cost. Items found in the recycling bin can become instant ingredients for inventing and building something new. Plain paper and a few crayons can create a runway for toy airplanes or a race track for cars. Blankets thrown over a few chairs or a table can become an indoor fort or tent. If you have home Internet access, take advantage of the countless printable coloring sheets and activities available online, completely free and available at a moment's notice.

Get More from What You Have

Do your children often seem bored with their toys or, worse, claim they have nothing to do despite their overflowing toy box? Don't tax your budget to buy more stuff.

Consider asking a friend to swap some toys with you. Each family can fill a box with toys the children no longer play with but are still in good condition and then trade boxes so each family gets the novelty of "new" toys without the expense.

Too many toys can overwhelm children and clutter a room. Stretch your toy-spending dollars by minimizing the need to buy new toys at all. Rotate toys so only certain ones are available at a time. Your child will let you know when it's time to bring out the "new" ones when he or she loses interest in what's already out.

Penny Pitfall

Don't be suckered into purchasing all the accompanying accessories for the latest, greatest toy. If accessories are truly needed, purchase them secondhand, create them yourself, or select accessories manufactured by a different, less-expensive brand.

Free up your budget while freeing up your children to entertain themselves by allowing them to play with the real thing once in a while. Does your little girl adore playing dress-up? Save some of your old clothing and costume jewelry just for her. Do you have a budding chef in the family? Allow him to use his imagination to whip up fabulous play with some pots and pans out of the kitchen. Take out the canned goods from the pantry and a few paper bags, and let the kids play grocery store.

When to Buy

If you're like most people, you purchase toys when you need them, around birthdays and at holiday times. If you wait until the last minute, though, you'll likely end up paying top dollar. Toy shelves, just like car lots and electronics departments, need to be cleared of old stock to make room for new incoming products. And as you might have guessed, new toys come out right around the holidays, just in time to entice kiddos into begging their parents to buy the latest and greatest— and often very expensive—toys.

Avoid this spending trap by buying toys during the clear-out period, during late summer and early fall. From around August until early October, toys regularly go on clearance for the express purpose of selling them quickly. Toy manufacturers ship truckloads of toys to stores well before this time so the shelves are stocked and ready before the onslaught of holiday toy advertising begins. Take advantage of stores' need to make more room, and keep more money in your pocket at the same time.

Putting off the inevitable can be costly and disappointing; if you're planning on purchasing your child the new "hot" toy of the season, pick it up when you see it. Procrastinating or thinking you might find it cheaper elsewhere later may mean you have a more difficult time finding it in a few weeks—or worse—you may not find it all or end up paying a premium for it if you do. If you're worried about missing out on a future sale price, tuck the receipt somewhere safe, continue to check the ads, and revisit the store with the receipt and unopened toy for a price adjustment later. Most stores honor sales prices during a 30- to 90-day period. Check with stores in your area to find out their specific policies before you buy.

Car Seats and Boosters for Less

Safety isn't necessarily tied to price when it comes to children's car seats and boosters. You obviously want to look for the safest options available, but don't make the assumption that the more expensive the price tag, the better the safety rating. The safest option is a car seat you'll use all the time—and use correctly. A car seat not installed or used properly isn't safe at all, no matter how hefty the price tag.

Super Saver _____

It's easy to get over-whelmed by the cost of infant car seats. Before you buy, call your local hospital or pediatrician's office for information on local discount programs. Many organizations help new parents find affordable car seats. Some organizations and hospitals even provide them for free!

Shop, shop, and shop some more to find a model you like at a price you're willing to pay. Visit a larger, trendy baby store that offers wide selection of seats and boosters and try out a number of different models, but keep your money tucked safely away. Instead, make a note of the exact name and model of the seat you prefer and then see if you can find it for less elsewhere, either in another store or online.

Prepurchase Considerations

You can also stretch your dollars by looking for car seats that grow or adjust with your child. It's important to select and use the correct seat for your child's size and weight, but did you realize that many seats and boosters adjust to lengthen the amount of time you can safely use them? It makes good dollar-stretching sense to spend a bit more money upfront to purchase a car seat or booster that will safely last longer.

If your family uses two cars, purposefully select a seat that can quickly, easily, and *safely* be removed, reinstalled, and used in all the vehicles your family uses.

The extras do count. You and your child will likely be living with this purchase for a long time, so be sure it works well for both of you. Removable and washable covers, cup holders, and arm and headrests all contribute to the overall comfort, durability, and function of a car seat. You may very well pay a bit extra for these additional features, but you're also less likely to regret the purchase.

How to Buy Secondhand Safely

Purchasing and using secondhand car seats is perfectly safe if you keep a few precautions in mind. It's never smart to trade safety for cents, but often babies and small children outgrow car seats so quickly it doesn't make sense to *not* take advantage of the possible savings. Use the following tips to stretch your dollars while ensuring you purchase the safest preowned car seat possible:

◆ Don't purchase car seats manufactured before January 1, 1981. (Strict federal safety standards went into effect on this date.) Better yet, avoid purchasing a car seat that's more than 5 years old.

◆ Verify that the car seat has never been involved in an accident. Car seats are manufactured to safely withstand only one crash. Even if the seat appears okay, looks can be deceiving. Don't chance it.

◆ No instructions? No manual? Don't buy it. For a car seat to adequately protect your little one, it must be installed properly. You probably can't do that without the manual.

◆ Look closely for obvious wear. If you see cracks, dents, or any missing parts, don't buy the car seat. If it looks like it hasn't been well taken care of, it probably hasn't.

◆ Check with the manufacturer beforehand to verify the car seat hasn't been recalled. To do this, you'll need the name, model number, and manufactured date. Many companies offer this information on their websites.

It's better to buy the best car seat you can possibly afford, new or used. Taking these few simple precautions, you can rest assured that your money will be well invested in your child's safety. Keep these in mind, too, if you'd like to sell your car seat when your child is too big to use it safely.

Less-Costly Furry-Friend Care

For many, the pitter patter of little feet makes a house a home. That includes feet of the furry variety, too. Pets, just like kids, enrich your life and warm your heart but can cost a pretty penny if you're not smart. Keep a tight leash on your pet-related spending with the following tips and tricks.

Trim Everyday Expenses

One easy way to stretch your pet-food dollars is to purchase larger packages of food. By buying in bulk, you can often afford to purchase higher-quality food, which contributes to your pet's overall good health. Cheaper pet food is cheap for a reason; it's often packed with inexpensive fillers such as by-products, corn, rice, wheat, and soy instead of nutrient-rich ingredients. Generally speaking, the more unpronounceable the ingredients, the more unhealthy they are for your pet.

You can also stretch your pet-food dollars by checking out the *unit prices* of the available brands. They're usually listed on the shelf sticker or tag underneath the package price in small print.

def•i•ni•tion

Unit price refers to the price per ounce, pound, or individual item, not the price per packaged amount. It's more indicative of value because it can help you better compare the available brands.

The easiest way to stretch your dollars while meeting your pet's needs is to find your own solutions. When buying a litter box for your cat, don't spend extra money to buy a plastic box just because it's labeled as such. Check out the storage section of any discount store, and you're sure to find a cheaper option that's just as functional.

Avoid spending money to buy cutesy but expensive food and water dishes. Not only are they more expensive, but they can be unsafe as well. Plain stainless steel is best, as other containers can harbor bacteria or even emit unhealthy gases. I guarantee your animal cares more about what's in the dish than what it looks like. Find your own containers at home to repurpose for your pet's use, or visit a thrift store to find what you need for less.

Pet stores are filled to the brim with expensive comfort items for pets in a plethora color options, trims, and textures. Truth be told, all those little extras are for you, not your pet, and you'll pay dearly for them. Keep your money and keep something out of the landfill, and give your pet an old blanket or towel to use in the carrier or pet bed. Even an old bed or throw pillow can make a great cushion for an animal carrier or bed.

Where toys are concerned, you can pay extra money to get your dog a new Frisbee at the pet store, or you can use the old one already in the garage. Your dog won't care.

For cats, don't waste money on cat toys when a string and an attentive owner will more than suffice. (Your cat will like playing with you better than playing alone, too!) Stretch the money you spend on catnip by containing the mess and making it last longer. Fill up an old sock and tie the end in a knot. If you've got a green thumb, grow your own catnip and save spending your bucks on the store-bought stuff.

 Penny Pitfall

> One word of caution when it comes to toys: don't give your dog an old shoe to use as a chew toy. Apart from the potential danger to your dog's health, it can cause confusion when you try to designate some shoes as chew toys and others as off-limits.

Health and Grooming Costs

Consider alternative ways to get your pet the vaccinations he needs. Visit a shot clinic sponsored by Animal Control, the Humane Society, or a pet store in your community. Your pet will get the same vaccine protection at a fraction of the cost. Some places also offer low-cost spay and neuter services. Check your local shelter or animal control.

Also worth noting for both your dog's health and your wallet is that the only shot required by law is the rabies vaccination. Other yearly shots for full-grown dogs are not required. Puppies should get the initial puppy series of shots, which are usually a set of three or four spaced a few weeks apart, but after that, additional vaccinations can actually be detrimental to your dog's health. Ask your vet for more information if this concerns you.

While most pet insurance policies don't cover the cost of routine care, it may still be worth considering to protect your budget from unnecessary strain should something happen to your pet's health. If your pet is older or if you would pay any amount to save your pet's life, a pet policy may be for you. In the event your dog or cat needs surgery, hospitalization, or treatment for a devastating health concern such as cancer, the relatively small payments you paid for the policy can shrink in comparison to the mounting medical bills the insurance company will pay instead of you.

> **Dollar Stretcher**
>
> Do you live near a veterinary school? If you do, find out what it offers in terms of pet care. They often have low-cost clinics where you can bring your pet for reduced fees.

There's no shame in taking a little time to think when deciding about high-priced vet recommendations. If you're at the vet only to have her suggest an expensive procedure, protect your money and your pet by asking for some time to think about it either there in the office or at home. Taking the pressure off and *not* making the decision in the heat of the moment can help you clarify your priorities and may even help you come up with another possible solution or resource.

Visiting a groomer can be stressful on your pet and your budget. Make grooming a more enjoyable process for your pet, and a less expensive one for you, by taking care of it at home. Invest in the proper products and tools to make your job easier as well as safer for your pet. Ask your vet or a pet store employee for suggestions.

If your pet takes maintenance medications, consider purchasing them online for substantial savings. Be careful to ensure that the cost of shipping doesn't trump your overall savings. Many online pet medication suppliers offer free shipping, but it's usually only if you purchase a certain amount.

A wise person once said that it's the little things in life that matter most. Ironically, it's often a home's smallest occupants who eat up a large portion of a household budget as well. Don't evict them; just tame the costs to keep everyone happy and well cared for while keeping a leash on unnecessary expenses.

Chapter 10

Keep Your Stomach *and* Your Wallet Full

In This Chapter

- ◆ Dollar-stretching meal-planning strategies
- ◆ Ways to "eat out" while eating in
- ◆ Eating out and spending less
- ◆ Stretch-savvy bill-lowering tips

The cost of food can be a huge household expense, especially with food prices rising ever higher. That's the bad news. The good news is that you decide how much money you need to spend on food. Whether you eat out, dine in, or order takeout, you can stretch your food dollars and get everything you want without feeling deprived!

Cut Food Costs at Home

No matter your dining preferences, the more processed, packaged, or prepared the food, the more you'll pay for it. This isn't necessarily a bad thing. There are certainly times when paying a premium for such convenience can still be a savings. When you're sicker than a dog, for example, and still have a family to feed, paying for and keeping a few frozen entrées on hand is far cheaper than ordering a pizza.

On the other hand, an easy way to stretch your food dollar while actually improving food quality is to tackle more of the prep work yourself. That doesn't have to mean forgetting the convenience factor, either.

Plan to create your own cost-effective convenience items by prepping foods you've purchased at a discount ahead of the time you need them. Use a large re-sealable plastic container or a baggy to store washed and cut lettuce for your own prepped salads. (Place a paper towel inside to whisk away excess moisture and keep the lettuce fresher longer.) Build your own frozen dinners by preparing foods such as homemade burritos, enchiladas, pizza bread, soups, stews, and chili in bulk and freeze smaller portions. You'll not only save quite a bit of money by creating your own prepped-ahead food, but you'll greatly decrease the amount of chemicals and preservatives in your foods as well.

Dollar $tretcher

Be sure you experience all the flavors with every meal: bitter, salty, sweet, sour, and pungent. If your taste buds are satisfied, you won't reach for snacks later. A satisfied palate goes a long way to a satisfied pocket book with the extra benefit of a trim belly, so think about the five flavors while you plan your meals.

Plan Ahead and Save

You know you're going to eat dinner every day, so why not plan your meals ahead of time and save money doing it? The great thing about meal planning is you can start off small and gradually increase the amount of effort involved to stretch your grocery dollars even more.

By planning your meals, you're not only less likely to succumb to the temptation to eat out (which can be expensive unless you follow the tips I share later in this chapter), but you can better avoid impulse purchases at the grocery store. Planning ahead also enables you to make better

use of what you already have in
your cupboards and minimize
what you need to purchase.

A little more involved but also
more financially rewarding is
planning your meals around sales
and coupons. The front and back
page of weekly sales fliers show all
the loss leaders. (Remember loss
leaders from Chapter 2?) Using
these as the key ingredients in
your meal planning will ensure
maximum value for food dollars.

 Super Saver

> If you're used to eating
> out or simply throwing meals
> together, start off by planning
> a few meals each week. As
> your money stretches further
> and your comfort level grows,
> begin tackling weekly and
> monthly menus you can then
> rotate.

Using coupons to help create meal plans can also stretch your bucks
and cut costs, especially when the store offers double or even triple coupons. Cash in coupons in conjunction with sale prices and compound
your savings even more. Hardcore dollar stretchers can even purchase
extra ingredients (at the reduced cost, of course) and prepare a double
or triple batch of a meal to freeze and use later. This not only stretches
your food dollars, but minimizes the amount of preparation per meal
and maximizes energy costs to cook it.

A Little Prep Work = Lots of Savings

Buying in bulk is a dollar-stretching no-brainer everyone can take
advantage of. Stretch your dollar by not paying a manufacturer to portion out, prep, and freeze food for you; do it yourself to save and get
even more food for your dollar.

The challenge, though, is making sure your bulk purchases don't spoil
before you can use them. That's wasteful twice, in food and in money.
Maintain food quality and save time and energy by preparing meals in
advance. Breaking down bulk purchases into meal-size portions saves
you time and energy later when all you have to do is heat and eat your
homemade TV dinner. This also reduces the temptation to eat out
because you don't have anything at home good to eat.

Afraid of freezer burn? There's no need to be, if you take a few preemptive steps. Although food that's been properly frozen never technically

Dollar $tretcher

If you're single, don't assume this dollar-stretching opportunity is only for families. You can easily prepare a meal that serves four and freeze the three remaining portions. Do this multiple times each week, and your freezer will be well stocked with quick, dollar-stretching dinner options in no time.

becomes unsafe to eat, it can lose its taste and texture over time, thanks to freezer burn, caused when cold air is trapped against the food. Prevent it by packaging your freezer items so the least amount of air comes in contact with the food as possible. (For more information on storing food in the freezer, see Resources.)

Vacuum sealers are ideal for this, but there are other, more economical solutions as well. Aluminum foil is great because it's readily available and can be molded directly to the shape of the food it's protecting. The empty waxed paper or plastic bags inside the cereal box is good for freezer food, too. Simply cut it flat, wipe it clean, and use it to rewrap items to keep in the freezer. It's free and excellent for helping stave off freezer burn. With a little practice, you can become an expert at freezing premade meals, stretching those dollars so you can buy quality ingredients to satisfy your taste buds!

Did you know that a full freezer is a happy freezer? The more items inside, the less energy it takes to keep the contents cold. This translates to lower electric bill. The more full the freezer, though, the more of a challenge it can be to shuffle through everything inside. Keep your freezer functioning well and easy to manage by using some of the same space ideas as you would use in your fridge. If you designate certain areas of your freezer to specific foods, you'll avoid guesswork and save electricity (and money) by not having to keep the freezer door open while you hunt for something.

To keep soups that contain pasta or rice at their best for second servings, separate tonight's dinner from tomorrow's leftovers while you're cooking. Only add the starch—the pasta or rice—to tonight's dinner, and freeze and store the remainder without it. Tomorrow (or whenever), simply thaw, heat, and add the pasta or rice for better quality and taste.

Another way to stretch your food dollar is simply not to waste it. While freezing and properly storing your food is key, so is making sure the food actually gets eaten later. Become a magician with leftovers.

Put them in a different dish and melt cheese over the top. Create special new toppers for soup such as thick slices of garlic bread with melted cheese or even a few salad croutons. Create a quick new side to serve along with yesterday's main dish today to help keep *leftovers* from becoming a dreaded word in your house. After all, the more disguised a leftover food, the more well received it will be, so add something new every time you serve it, and you'll keep your dinners happy.

Penny Pitfall

It almost never pays to purchase and prep fresh vegetables to freeze because you'll almost always find a similar or cheaper price for frozen vegetables on sale. So save your time and still stretch your dollar and buy frozen vegetables labeled "fancy" or "USDA Grade A." These are picked at the peak of freshness and quickly frozen for best taste.

Eat "Out" at Home

Dining out has so much appeal. Yummy food. No preparation. Nearly no clean-up. But it does cost money. You can still get the ease and convenience of dining out by dining out at home. Plus, you save money by not having to leave a tip!

Takeout is a great compromise between preparing meals at home and eating out. If you're a frequent takeout diner at a specific restaurant, own up to it. Program the restaurant's phone number into your cell phone to avoid paying the cost of calling directory assistance each time.

And be sure to get the same bang for your buck. If a side of bread is usually served alongside a salad inside the restaurant, ask if you can also get it with your takeout order. Don't forget to ask for extra portions of the sauces and dressings as well. If you're ordering an entrée that includes it to begin with, you usually won't be charged extra, and you'll be left with more to enjoy later.

Dollar $tretcher

Should you tip for takeout orders, or keep those dollars in your pocket? Unless the person who took your order went above and beyond in some way, you don't have to tip. After all, you'll be bussing your own table at home.

There's an even more economical way to eat "out" at home. If you've successfully dissected any meal at a restaurant, you've probably discovered that they can't cook pasta or prepare meat or chop vegetables better than you can do it at home. Chances are it's the sides, sauces, and little extras that make the restaurant's meals such a treat. You can eat well and still stretch your bucks by ordering your takeout in a creative way.

For example, instead of ordering an entire entrée, order a small container of the accompanying sauce. Some restaurants have already caught on and now cater to this dollar-stretching crowd of diners by selling their own secret sauces, salad dressings, and spices bottled for such purchases.

Another great way to eat well while dining in is to use the Internet. Countless websites are devoted to revealing the recipes of successful restaurants. Whether posted by a disgruntled employee seeking revenge or simply a die-hard fan who has successfully unlocked the culinary secrets through trial and error, many recipes are out there just waiting to be found. Simply open any search engine and run a search on the name of the entrée, the name of the restaurant, and the word *recipe*.

Eating Out for Less

Now that you know how to eat in for less, don't think you can't still eat out while stretching your dollar. There are countless ways to make eating out far less expensive than you might think. Arm yourself with the tips and tricks in this section, and you can navigate the traps of hungry children, order exactly what you want for less, and still leave with a full tummy.

Choose Your Restaurant Wisely

Before deciding on a restaurant based only on what sounds good, consider all your options. Different restaurants have different strengths. To evaluate these strengths, consider the following:

- *Speed of service.* Will you have to wait long for a table or for your order? The longer the wait, the more tempted your hungry tummy will be to want to order expensive add-ons to your meal such as appetizers and salads.

♦ *Extra accommodations.* Does the restaurant provide activities for children? Do they provide free appetizers?

♦ *Accuracy.* Does the restaurant have a good track record of getting your order right?

♦ *Variety.* Does the restaurant provide enough choices in the menu to keep everyone in your party happy?

Taking the time to evaluate all your restaurant choices also helps you avoid making costly snap decisions. A restaurant with higher prices might actually be more of a value if you take all the extras into consideration. Such a restaurant might have larger portions that enable you to take the leftovers with you for lunch tomorrow or may offer complimentary bread service while you wait.

Super Saver

Don't let your server sweet-talk you into ordering a beverage other than water if water's what you want. If he or she returns with what may as well be a shot glass–size serving of water, ask for a larger glass or even a pitcher to be left at the table.

It Pays to Be Creative

More and more restaurants are catering to parties with a variety of dining interests. The more food options and price points an restaurant can offer, the greater their chances of luring you (and your money) in. This can easily work to the advantage of a super dollar stretcher like you.

Don't take what the menu shows at face value. Many ethnic restaurants have a small portion of the menu dedicated to traditional American fare. Ironically, this can be much cheaper than what you'd find in traditional American restaurants. Next time you're in the mood for a good burger, consider visiting a Mexican restaurant instead and enjoy the free chips and salsa, too.

There's nothing worse than getting seated only to realize there's nothing affordable on the menu. Many restaurants post their menus online as well as outside their restaurants, so check those out ahead of time to find out where your money will stretch the most.

Penny Pitfall

If you're dining out with friends, agree ahead of time to get separate bills or go dutch. Whatever you do, don't agree to simply divide the total bill evenly among the number in your party; otherwise, your inexpensive salad could turn into a real budget-buster.

The menu prices of some items may seem high at first glance, but you can often divide the portion between two or more people and conquer the final bill. Remember: think, divide, and conquer! Get creative. Even salad portions can be more than generous, so consider ordering one salad and one entrée, for example, and split both, or add a side of meat such as grilled chicken or shrimp to a dinner salad to make it heartier yet less expensive than actually ordering a larger salad or entrée.

You've probably heard that you should never grocery-shop hungry, and the same applies to restaurants. Be wary of looking at a menu while your stomach is screaming to be fed. Many dollars have been squandered by such overordering. Have an idea of what you'd like to order before you even open the menu. Someone got paid big bucks to write those mouth-watering descriptions. Just be sure you're not handing over your bucks needlessly.

Here are just a few ideas to get your creative, dollar-stretching juices flowing on how to fill your stomach without emptying your wallet:

♦ Consider ordering appetizers and large salads as entrées.

♦ Ask your server if the restaurant has a *split plate charge* before you order one dish for two of you.

♦ Build your own meal by picking and choosing from sides or à la carte items. (More tips on à la carte items later in the chapter.)

♦ Inquire if a complimentary *baby plate* or children's appetizer is available.

♦ Frequent restaurants that offer "Kids Eat Free" promotions. The price of adult entrées can be a real value if they come along with free kid meals.

♦ Eat at off-peak times for better service *and* better prices. Restaurants often offer special pricing during slow periods on various days of the week and/or hours of the day to bring in business.

♦ Avoid all-inclusive pricing. If you weren't planning on ordering a beverage, side salad, or dessert, be sure you're not paying for it. Some restaurants include these in the price of the meal.

♦ Go to a BYOB (bring your own bottle) restaurant and save the money on wine or beer. You still get the great atmosphere at a fraction of the cost! (Though do inquire ahead of time if there's a corking charge!)

♦ Go out to lunch instead of dinner. Most restaurants have the same great menu at a fraction of the price.

♦ If you know the restaurant serves large portions, ask to have half of it immediately boxed up to take home with you. Voilà, two meals for the price of one!

def•i•ni•tion

Split plate charge is an extra fee applied to the bill when only one entrée is ordered and then shared. Sometimes the extra charge includes an extra side item or salad. Other times, you'll merely get an extra plate and you'll be asked to do the dividing yourself. Baby plate refers to a small, often complimentary, plate of food provided for a baby or a young child while the adults place and wait for their order. Baby plates are usually not advertised but are often provided upon request.

If you're visiting a new restaurant, be sure to ask your wait staff about portion size. They can help guard you against ordering more food than you need and subsequently keep your bill in check. The wait staff may also have some ideas to help stretch your bucks even more. A friendly smile and an honest query about any special pricing can go a long way to making your final bill as small as possible. Your server, after all, is the person who will be ringing up your bill. He might very well know of a better way to order the same thing for a cheaper price. Feel like splurging on that plate of onion rings, but don't quite feel like paying full price? Tell your server. He might be able to order you a half portion that isn't advertised on the menu for less money.

Hungry, Hungry Kiddos

It seems ironic: the very reason many of us are so busy and seek the time and sanity saving refuge of a restaurant is the very same reason eating out can be so expensive—*kids!* It's oh so very tempting to just allow the wee ones to order whatever they want so they order quickly. The faster that plate of food gets in front of their faces, the better. Anyone who has children (or has dined anywhere near them) understands that simple truth. Fortunately, though, dining out with children does not have to be such a costly experience.

To help keep the kiddos *at* the table instead of *under* it, be prepared. In your dining out arsenal, be sure to include the following:

♦ Small, portable, sure-fire snacks from home to satisfy small appetites while ordering and waiting.

♦ Activity ideas. Know in advance whether or not the restaurant provides crayons or some other activity. If not, bring your own. Boredom can be costly!

♦ Your child's silverware from home. Smaller, child-size spoons and forks help ensure more of the food you're paying for ends up in their mouth rather than on the floor.

♦ Bibs. Bibs not only keep food from reaching the floor, but help protect another costly investment—the child's clothing.

Initially, this list may seem like more work than simply eating at home. On the other hand, a large re-sealable plastic baggie works great to contain all these items and can be left in the car for quick trips out to restaurants. As you'll see, having these things handy when you need them helps ensure your dining experience with your children stretches only your dollars and not your sanity.

Eating out can be equally as difficult with older children as it is with the younger crowd. Depending on your child's age and math ability, you can employ your child's skills and interests in helping minimize the final bill. Share your meal budget with him, and explain how much he may spend on his order. Set a dollar limit, and tell him that everything he orders must add up to no more than the allotted amount. Not only will this help ensure your budget remains intact, but it reinforces his mental math skills, honors his individuality, and builds his self-esteem by enabling him to become more independent.

Tricks to Minimize Your Restaurant Bill

Like any good book, menus have a beginning, a middle, and an end. However, don't read it in that order. Take a good look at all appetizers, entrées, *à la carte* items, and desserts before making your selection. You may very well find that what you had planned on ordering as an entrée is also listed as a smaller, less-expensive appetizer. If you feel like a smaller portion would satisfy you, go for it. You can also skip directly to the à la carte section of the menu and order a side or two as your meal.

Another way to tackle a menu is to quickly scan it for your price point. Everyone has a price he or she's willing to pay for something, especially a dollar stretcher. If you know in advance how much you're willing to spend on the meal, you can quickly whittle down your options by simply scanning the menu for items in your price range. Don't forget to ask the wait staff for any unadvertised specials, and remember to glance at the *fresh sheet*, or "today's specials," which often advertises limited time offers or special pricing.

Can't find exactly what you want on the menu? Don't assume the restaurant doesn't have it or can't make it. In fact, being creative with your ordering—when done politely—can often be a rewarding experience in more ways then

def•i•ni•tion

À la carte is French for "from the card" and describes items that are priced separately and can be ordered individually. **Fresh sheet** is a smaller menu available at restaurants in addition to the main menu. The fresh sheet changes frequently and often features special items at a significant savings.

one. Not only do you stand to get exactly what you want, but you might even get it at a cheaper price.

For example, it never hurts to ask if you, too, may order off the children's menu. Even if the restaurant wants to charge you for an adult-size portion, you still may be able to rake in substantial savings versus the conventional menu pricing. Often the portions are ample enough even for an adult, and many come with more nutritious side options such as apple slices or mandarin oranges in lieu of fries.

Don't Pay Full Price

Avoid paying for what you don't want. Only a portion of an entrée sound good? Be sure to ask if it's available alone as a side. If you're a vegetarian or simply prefer a menu item without the meat, don't be shy about asking for a small discount to reflect that.

Coupons can be a cash cow when you're eating out. You can find these little money-savers anywhere, from the back of cash register receipts to newspapers to online. If you can plan ahead, you can save big time by hunting down a discount prior to dining. Just be sure to present your coupon to the wait staff before ordering to ensure it will be honored. Read the fine print, and beware of coupon requirements as well. Some discounts and coupons may only be redeemable at certain times and with certain purchases.

 Super Saver

> Got a coupon that requires the purchase of two entrées, but dining alone? Outsmart the fine print! Order two different entrées to meet the requirement, and still take advantage of the coupon savings. Enjoy one meal dining in at the restaurant, and have the second boxed to take home for a later meal.

Also beware of coupons that have certain purchase requirements. If a coupon requires you to order a certain amount of items that you weren't going to order in the first place, it's really not such a great deal after all.

"Check, Please!"

The best way to ensure you enjoy your meal is to avoid the sticker-shock-induced indigestion when you receive the bill. Nothing is worse than seeing an inflated number you weren't expecting. It helps it keep a mental tab running of what you should owe at the end of a meal so you're not only aware of what you're spending, but also so any errors will be more apparent.

Of course it's part of your server's job to try to keep you in the restaurant for as long as possible. The longer you're there, the more likely you are to order and eat more. Another drink, maybe dessert, possibly a cup of coffee—it all adds up. Don't wait until you're completely finished with your meal to ask for the bill. Ask for it after you've received the last thing you're planning to order. By doing this, you'll give your wait staff plenty of time to get the bill printed and give yourself ample time to have any errors corrected. Plus, you'll be less likely to waste time sitting around waiting—or worse, inadvertently paying the incorrect amount simply to make a swift exit.

 Super Saver

Place your wallet or purse up on the table or hold up your credit card for your server to see to let him know you're ready for the bill. But never allow your card to be charged until you've looked at the final total.

Whether you're dining in or dining out, keep your dollar-stretching skills handy to keep your tummy full and your wallet fat.

Chapter 11

Stretching Your Entertainment Dollar

In This Chapter

◆ Get the most from entertainment discounts

◆ Cut costs without sacrificing fun

◆ Easy ways to make staying home more enjoyable

◆ Stretch-savvy ways to splurge

A cheapskate hoards his money. A dollar stretcher spends her money wisely to live well. You work hard for your money, so make the money you earn work even harder to help you play. It's easy to have fun and still stay within your budget when you do it with an eye toward getting more for less. In this chapter, you discover how to stretch your entertainment dollar to the max.

More Bang for Your Entertainment Buck

Sometimes the biggest key to stretching your dollar is to simply be flexible. Often you can find great deals in entertainment if you don't insist on planning too far ahead. For instance, you can wait and purchase tickets for performances at the last minute. You run the risk of the show being sold out, but you also stand to take advantage of any last-minute savings the venue offers. Any business would rather get something for a seat rather than nothing. So flexibility can go a long way toward getting you some good, cheap fun!

Don't forget that many popular places also offer discounts. Consider touring museums, zoos, and galleries on designated discount days. You may be limited in the days and times you can choose to visit, but you'll stretch your money further by doing so.

Enjoy Your Favorite Outings for Less

Here's some good news: there's dollar-stretching strength in numbers. Museums, concerts, and even movie theatres often offer group discounts. Why not consider getting a bunch of friends or family together to share in the fun and the savings? It may take longer to plan the outing, but a bigger group means you can also take advantage of carpooling and save on gas and possible parking costs. Then, you can spend that savings on snacks, or pocket the extra cash for your next outing.

Instead of going to dinner and a movie, consider going to a movie and then dinner. If you go to a matinee and have dinner afterward, you'll save on the movie tickets. You can then spend more on dinner, or squirrel away the extra loot.

Penny Pitfall

Don't waste your money on a movie that isn't worth it. If you can't get into it or if an unruly baby or child is ruining your experience, get up and leave. If you exit the theater within the first 10 or 15 minutes and see the manager, you can usually get complimentary passes for your next visit.

Always be ready to ask for and take advantage of any affiliation, student, or senior discounts by having the appropriate ID ready at all times. Does your company ID get you into any venues at a discount? Many big companies have such arrangements, so check out yours.

If you frequent a place often and a membership is available, pay the higher price upfront to join. Better to own up to the fun now and pay for the membership than to get nickeled and dimed when you add up the cost of all the individual visits. Additional perks and savings might be available only to card-carrying members, such as free parking, special admission days and hours, and discounts off affiliated purchases, adding even more value to the membership. A frequent flyer program might earn you free popcorn or even free movie tickets.

Cut Your Costs Even More

Before you go out anywhere, get online. Many venues and businesses offer online ticket sales so you can buy ahead of time and skip long waits in line once you arrive. You'll often find web-only savings as well. Check that there are no fees involved, however.

Local libraries are completely free, and many libraries work hard to keep their book, movie, and CD collections up-to-date. You may have to wait a bit longer to enjoy a newly released movie, but taking advantage of any waitlist or holding system can help shorten that wait. Our local library often holds movie night. Free movies for the whole family!

Spend a bit of money upfront to invest in saving money on fun adventures throughout the year. Visit www.entertainment.com or call 1-888-231-SAVE (1-888-231-7283) to purchase an Entertainment book full of coupons for all sorts of fun outings specific to your area. If the cost is more than you want to spend alone, share the fun and split the cost by finding a friend willing to go in on the purchase with you.

Dollar $tretcher

Volunteering is fun, free, and commendable. Find a cause you believe in and do something you enjoy for a sure-fire win-win situation. From spending time playing with animals at your local shelter to landscaping local parks, the possibilities are endless.

Don't feel like paying for coupons? Many online coupon sites are now offering free, printable coupons for all different kinds of entertainment opportunities. Check out www.valpak.com and www.coolsavings.com and click the entertainment links to find out more.

Affordable Ways to Splurge

Great things often do come in small packages, and big splurges can come with small price tags, too. Know what you enjoy and what makes you feel pampered, so you can treat yourself in a way that doesn't feel like you're skimping even though you may not be shelling out a lot of money.

Consider investing in products that have lasting splurging power. If you enjoy the relaxation of paraffin wax treatments at the spa, for example, spend the money on the one-time purchase to equip yourself with your own machine at home. Enjoy massages? Purchase your own massaging mat to place over a chair in your home to enjoy whenever you like.

If fancy coffee drinks with great foam are your thing, a small, inexpensive electronic whip can give you great froth over and over again for a minimal one-time cost. A friend of ours was spending a fortune on lattes every day at her local coffee shop. Her husband bought her a cappuccino machine for Christmas, and now she's enjoying lattes from the comfort of her own couch. Although the machine was a one-time pricey layout, over time, they figured they'll save hundreds of dollars by not dishing out $5 bucks a day for specialty coffees.

Spoil Yourself Now and Then

If it improves the quality of your life by reducing stress, improving your health, or making your life easier, it isn't a splurge. Know when to spend money to make your life better so stretching your money in other areas is worth it and easier to do.

You don't have to shell out a lot of money to feel like you've spoiled yourself. Savor simplicity. A favorite coffee drink can be a mini vacation. Skip the spa and lounge in your own bathtub filled with indulgent bubbles and surrounded with scented candles. No one knows what you enjoy more than you do, so employ the expert—you!—and save some money to boot.

Use the following list of ideas as a springboard for finding new ways to splurge without spending a fortune. Your mental health will thank you, and you'll even have money left over to treat yourself more often!

- Ready for some new clothing or new jewelry? Find a group of friends and start a clothing or jewelry swap. Everyone leaves with new things to love without spending a dime, and you get to enjoy the company, too.

- Craving some new tunes? Don't purchase an entire CD, especially if you don't know if you'll like all the songs anyway. Purchase and download specific songs instead. Your money will stretch further, and you'll be sure only to get the songs you'll listen to again and again.

- Treat yourself to flowers, and don't wait for someone else to get around to doing it. Purchase a small bunch of cut flowers for your home or your desk at work. (Or pick your own from your garden for free!)

- Satisfy your sweet tooth by purchasing a pint of indulgent ice cream at the grocery store or a scoop at a local ice cream shop. Don't share it with anyone!

- Visit a high-end cosmetics or bath and body shop and sample all the luxurious products.

Sometimes all you need is a small pick-me-up. Taking the time and spending the money to treat yourself every now and again makes your life more enjoyable and you'll also be more productive and probably much more fun to be around.

Big Fun for a Small Price

New experiences bring a breath of fresh air to the daily grind. Bring your life to a halt for some much-needed fun with these dollar-stretching ideas of what to do for less:

- Dress up and visit an expensive restaurant for dessert only to enjoy an extravagant outing and great ambiance without paying the high cost.

◆ Explore a new culture without paying the high price of international travel. Travel with your taste buds by visiting an authentic ethnic restaurant in your area, or use the Internet to seek out new recipes from a variety of cultures to try at home.

◆ For a quick, rejuvenating vacation without the hefty price tag, consider staying overnight or spending the weekend at a local hotel. You'll get the same great hotel amenities as well as a change of scenery without having to pay the expense cost of long-distance travel.

◆ Get an inexpensive mini-makeover by visiting a local hair salon for a shampoo, blow-dry, and style. Who says you have to wait until your next haircut to enjoy a new look?

◆ Go ahead and schedule a massage; just cut the cost by opting for a shorter period of time or opt for a scalp- or neck-only massage.

Any experience that leaves you feeling like a million bucks is worth every penny. Experiences that don't cost that much, however, will leave you feeling even better. So go ahead, treat yourself well. Just be sure you treat your checkbook well at the same time.

Reinvent Staying at Home

Home is where the heart is, so make it a fun place to hang your hat, too. A bit of planning and an effort to stretch your creativity can go a long way toward making home the place you'd not only rather be, but the place you *want* to be.

Make staying in as much fun as possible by uncovering new ways to make the ho-hum anything but. Make having a fire at home a fun surprise by roasting marshmallows in the living room. It can be rainy outside, but make it fun indoors by having a meal on a blanket-covered floor picnic-style. For more grown-up fun, create your own murder mystery party by finding scripts online or writing your own. You're only limited by your own imagination, so get thinking to create more fun at home.

Making Home More Fun

Invest some of your entertainment dollars in making your home a more fun place to be. Stock your closets with great board games, new and retro. Purchase unique cookware, stemware, and serving ware to bring new life to meals and parties. A video game console can be a real value if it provides lasting enjoyment at home.

If you love movies but the cost is eating a hole in your wallet, consider joining a DVD movie club. Netflix (www.netflix.com) and Blockbuster (www.blockbuster.com) enable consumers to order movies directly from their computer and have them delivered to their mailbox within days. For a small monthly fee, movie lovers never have to leave their home, never incur late fees, and never have to pay return postage. Blockbuster offers the added convenience of allowing members to trade DVDs in immediately at any of their stores for another movie currently on the shelf.

 Super Saver

Start a video game lending library with your friends and co-workers. You can gain the fun of playing a variety of games without the huge investment.

Both Netflix and Blockbuster also offer immediate movie downloads on their sites. This means a plethora of movies available to members with just a point and click. Don't feel like watching a movie at your computer? No problem! Connect your TV directly to your computer as if it were your monitor instead. (Find cables for this purpose at any electronics store specializing in computers or audio/video supplies.)

Like the idea of a book club, but looking for something a bit more social? Start a movie club with friends. Decide on a monthly theme and meet weekly to enjoy a film together related to that month's theme. At the end of the month, meet again to discuss the various films.

Cabin-Fever-Fighters for Kids

Simply staying home more can be key to helping you stretch your dollar. If your household contains a few children, though, those four walls holding you all in can often become stifling with boredom. There's lots you can do to stave off the urge to jump in the car and keep cabin fever at bay.

Create messages with your own homemade invisible ink. Dissolve baking soda in warm water, and apply your message to paper using a paint brush or Q-tip. To reveal your message, paint over the paper with grape juice.

Take turns playing a timed version of the alphabet game. Set a timer and clock how long it takes each family member to find every letter of the alphabet in order somewhere in the house. For a real challenge, do it backward from Z to A!

Turn out all the lights, pull the curtains, and have a campfire in the living room. Use crumpled up red and yellow construction paper with a flashlight in the middle to "build" a fire. Tell ghost stories and sing songs.

Separate the children to different areas of the room so they're unable to see what each other is working on. Pass out paper and coloring supplies, turn on some music, and ask them to quietly draw whatever the music makes them think of. Compare all the pictures at the end to see how differently they interpreted the music visually.

Find and print free coloring sheets from various children's websites.

Pull a variety of items out of the recycle bin and challenge your children to invent or build something new. Broaden the activity by encouraging them to create an advertisement for their new creation.

Rip different colors of construction paper into small pieces and then use the "tiles" to create a mosaic.

Encourage your children to create a play. Spend time creating the set, building costumes, and even making tickets for the performance.

Dollar $tretcher

If you have small children, visit an "urban zoo" (a.k.a., a pet store) to enjoy watching fish, birds, and a multitude of small furry animals for absolutely free.

Let your children play with some food but then make them eat it! Use peanut butter or toothpicks to keep structures together, and provide a plethora of tasty, nutritious food to choose from such as raisins, carrot sticks, apple slices, and celery.

Play hopscotch in the house by using numbered pieces of paper on the floor.

Have each child hide some kind of treasure for the other children to find. After each child has hidden his or her treasure, ask them to write out clues or draw a map to their hidden treasure.

Pull out cushions, chairs, boxes, and blankets to build a good old-fashioned fort.

Have each child find four different items from throughout the house: three that are somehow the same and one that's different. Take turns trying to find out which item is the oddball in each set.

Donate some of your old magazines or recycled newspapers to an art cause and let your children create collages by cutting up the images to create their own.

Your children's imaginations have the ability to ignite fun no matter where they are, home included. Stretch your dollar by employing them to create their own entertainment rather than depending on someone, something, or somewhere else.

Where to Find Great Local Fun

When you live and work in an area, it can be easy to take it for granted. If you explore your area through the eyes of a tourist, you'll not only gain a new appreciation for where you live, but you'll likely have a whole lot of affordable fun while doing it. Rediscover what your state and local community has to offer, and open a whole new window to fun in your own backyard.

For example, contact your local office of travel and tourism to get all sorts of free information about different things to do in your state. You'll soon receive a bounty of resources such as maps of state parks, brochures for attractions, and even coupons for local businesses hoping to draw in visitor business.

College campuses can be a great resource for inexpensive entertainment. From concerts and plays to lectures and games, there's an endless supply of low-cost entertainment available to anyone willing to come on campus. Check college and university websites for event information and admission fees.

Keep your eyes peeled and your ears open for free concerts, movies, or plays in local parks. Frequent bars and restaurants that feature the talent of local artists. Even if they require a cover charge, you'll likely enjoy a great evening at an even better price.

Ask your local parks and recreation department for a schedule of classes and activities. Learn a new skill, have fun, and make new friends all at the same time.

State fairs can provide great entertainment. You'll likely be charged admission, but if you stay clear of the rides, you can enjoy hours of enjoyment browsing the exhibits, animals, and decked-out fairgrounds.

Dollar $tretcher

Get big-league fun for a fraction of the cost by checking out minor league, college, and high school games and sporting events. Not only are admission and ticket prices less expensive, but parking is often free and the money you spend on concessions may actually go toward a worthwhile cause such as funding sports programs for young adults.

If you live in an apartment complex, you're likely already paying for great entertainment possibilities, so take advantage of them. Sports courts, swimming pools, gyms, recreation rooms, and hot tubs are all commonplace in many complexes. Make the time to enjoy it.

Local martial arts, dance studios, and cultural centers often provide free demonstrations for community members. Check their websites for more information. Even many plant nurseries offer free or low-cost classes to help cultivate your green thumb (and hopefully new business for them).

Sure, money doesn't buy happiness, but it can make having fun easier. The trick is to find different ways to have fun across the spending spectrum. Know when it's possible to have just as much fun while skimping so you're left with extra money when you want to splurge. If your entertainment arsenal is well equipped with a variety of fun activities, regardless of cost, you'll never be bored—or broke!

Chapter 12

Have Suitcase–and Budget–Will Travel

In This Chapter

- ◆ Getting travel discounts
- ◆ Finding new places to stay
- ◆ Acquiring airline tickets for less
- ◆ Saving on the road

You might think you can't stretch your dollars and still take vacations. Well, you're wrong! Making your travel dollar stretch doesn't mean you have to resolve to be a recluse. From booking your flight, to packing, to while-you're-there considerations, your money-stretching smarts can help make your trip a success for you and your bottom line.

Vacation Without Emptying Your Wallet

It might seem impossible to be able to stretch travel dollars because there's so much expense involved with travel (and this might be the one time you want a little luxury). But you don't have to stay in hostels to make your travel dollars go further. It doesn't matter if you're traveling for fun or for necessity, the cost is the same. Take steps and heed a few words of caution before you go anywhere to help alleviate some of the extra expense. Your leftover money can go toward a splurge!

The most successful way to get the most for your travel dollars is to remain flexible. No matter how much money you saved booking your trip last time, there's no guarantee that's still the most economical way. Outsmart the high cost of travel by checking out different options to book your travel and accommodations. The more options you have, the greater your chances for big savings.

Unless you're a business traveler, your planned escapes are likely for leisure. Make flexibility your key to getting more bang for your traveling bucks. Airlines, hotels, and cruises know you have a choice and often do everything in their power to sway you to use their services rather than their competition's. Always shop around, and don't make a travel choice based on your first-glance prices. Find out what complementary extras are available. A hotel price may initially seem high but can be a real value if a complementary brunch is included, for example. One airline ticket price might be more expensive than another, but it might save you time and money by not requiring a layover or a connecting flight.

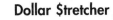

Dollar $tretcher

If you're traveling to a big city, plan your stay during the weekends when business travelers are gone and hotel rates go down. If you're visiting a traditional vacation or leisure destination, plan to visit during the week to save.

Getting Away for Less

Especially when you're traveling to a new or remote destination, consider using a travel agent's services. Traditional travel agents can provide the invaluable service of ensuring your trip is a successful, problem-free one. You may or may not pay a fee for their service, but they can save you money and frustration by anticipating and protecting you from any number of situations that may arise. If the hotel doesn't have your reservation or the rental place has no cars when you arrive, a quick call to your agent and you have someone to deal with the hassle. Travel agents are also highly specialized professionals. Employing their expertise may very well uncover other ways to save on your trip that you otherwise might not have thought of.

If you have time to do some digging for a deal yourself, pull up to your computer and search any of the many online discount travel sites. Many offer the comfort of traveling via a major company while still providing a great price. To minimize the hassle and time required to comparison-shop all the various travel sites, try using a travel search engine to help narrow your choices. (Find a list of discount travel sites and travel search engines in Resources.)

Penny Pitfall

Purchase nonrefundable tickets with caution. Oftentimes the lower the price, the more rigid the conditions. If there's any chance your plans may change, you may be stuck with a hefty fine in addition to the inconvenience. Research any rescheduling fees ahead of time and ensure that the savings is still worth the risk.

You could also buy travel insurance that will cover you if the trip falls through for some reason. Check out different travel insurance providers for the best rate.

Stretch-Savvy Ways to Stay

Your home away from home needn't burst your budget, either. The Internet, again, can help you save on where you stay. Visit travel sites or, if you have a specific hotel in mind, check out the hotel's website before making your reservation to look for web-only deals. (For a list of discount hotel sites, check out Resources.)

If you're calling the hotel directly, stretch your dollars even more by purposefully mentioning your coupon or discount code *after* the hotel quotes you their best rate. Unless the coupon or discount specifically states "not to be combined with any other discount or offer," you're likely to be able to compound your savings. If not, you're still better able to pick and choose which rate is the better of the two.

Don't forget to check with any organizations to which you may be a member. AAA and many professional organizations often enable you to get an extra discount.

If you're feeling a bit more adventurous, you may want to try home exchange. Home exchange enables regular people living in different parts of the world to literally exchange homes for a set period of time. While many sites that help facilitate home exchanges do charge membership fees, you don't pay for the accommodations themselves, as someone else is likely taking advantage of the same arrangement in your home. Often you're able to preview the home via photos posted online as well as read complete descriptions written by the owners.

While it's important to remember that you won't have any maid service during your stay, it's even more important to remember that you're staying in someone's home. If you're worried about someone trashing your home while you're away, remember they're likely having the same worries about you. On the other hand, there's peace of mind knowing your home is not completely empty, especially if you're gone for an extended period of time. If you're someone who normally hires a house-sitter, this can save you even more money. For more information on home exchange programs, visit www.intervac.com or www.homeexchange.com.

Super Saver

Visit Craigslist.org, choose your destination city, and click on "vacation rentals" in the "housing" section to check out lodging options made available by private homeowners. This can be an exceptional dollar-stretching solution, especially for large families or groups.

Cut Airline Costs

No one is immune to the ever-increasing cost of gas, airlines included. Unfortunately, that translates to higher ticket prices and extra fees for passengers. (And we've all noticed that when the gas prices go down again, the travel costs do not!) Fortunately, there are ways to make air travel more affordable. The more prepared and flexible you are, the more dollar-stretching success you'll experience.

More and more airlines are limiting the number of flights available and booking them to full capacity. This increases the chances of over-booked flights. If there's wiggle room in your travel time, consider allowing the airline to bump you to a different flight in exchange for travel vouchers to use in the future. If you do, don't forget to ask for a seat upgrade on your next flight as well. You may very well be able to finagle a first-class seat for free.

Dollar $tretcher

When you fly has as much control over the cost as where you're going. Consider traveling mid-week to take advantage of discounted rates carriers offer to entice more travelers during this traditionally slow time.

Getting Cheaper Tickets

If you want to fly with a specific airline, visit its website rather than calling to purchase your ticket. If you book the flight yourself, you save the airline time and money by not requiring extra assistance, and it passes this savings on to you via special online-only pricing.

Don't let being shy cost you savings. Call the airline and specifically ask about travel suggestions that will lead to a better-priced ticket. The ticket agent may be able to suggest a specific day of the week, time of the day, or connecting flights that can save you a substantial amount of money. Just be sure to hang up before you purchase the ticket. Make a note of the flight information and then book your own tickets online.

The same goes if you have questions. Go ahead and call, but then get off the phone and book your ticket online.

Unless you're looking at the flight as part of the vacation experience itself, be willing to skip some of the frills to save money. The flight, after all, is merely a means to an end—where you're going. Don't allow the cost of tickets to eat up all your fun money. Opt for an *ultra-low-cost carrier* (ULCC), and you'll see a huge difference in price. Being willing to do a little legwork yourself can save you money, too. Purposefully selecting a combination of connecting flights may require more effort on your part, but the overall savings may be worth it.

def•i•ni•tion

An **ultra-low-cost carrier** (ULCC) is an airline that charges travelers only for the services they use. Extras such as meal services and beverages, for example, are available, but for an additional charge. Ticket prices are kept low because the ticket price is not all-inclusive.

Spending Less at the Airport

Many airlines now levy an additional charge for each piece of baggage you check. Take precautions to protect your budget by strategically packing your bags. Fold or roll your clothing and place into re-sealable plastic bags. Partially close the bag and then roll up the bag or squeeze the bag tightly to push out all the excess air. Then close the bag completely. The more successful you are at compacting all your belongings, the less likely you are to have to pay for extra baggage.

If you're planning a lengthy stay, it may be worth it to invest in clothing that's less bulky and will take up less space in your suitcase.

Another option is to avoid packing in excess entirely. Being open to doing a load of laundry while you're traveling can significantly lower how much you have to pack to begin with. The small cost and inconvenience of doing a bit of laundry on the road can stretch your budget by more than just a few bucks, especially if you're traveling as a family.

Be forewarned: many airlines limit the amount of weight per piece of baggage. Check with the airline you're flying to be sure you don't get hit with a hefty overweight-luggage surcharge!

Dollar $tretcher

Most airlines allow passengers one piece of carry-on luggage and one personal item. Make the best use of the permissible personal item by using a backpack. You may find that you're less likely to have to pay for and use checked luggage, saving you money. If you're traveling with small children, they're entitled to the same carry-on allowances, so be sure to use them.

If, despite all your planning and careful packing, you're told you'll need to check (and pay for) your bag, don't immediately concede. Step aside and rearrange your bag a bit. Reducing some of the bulging in the outside pockets or squishing a few things into your purse, backpack, or even into the bag of someone else you're traveling with can save you money and hassle.

If this doesn't work, it may be worth it to throw away small toiletries or other items if you can pick them up relatively cheaply and conveniently at your destination. Hotels, after all, are catering more and more to traveler conveniences by providing complimentary toiletries and other small necessities. If it'll be available to you free at your destination, it makes more sense to toss it now and save your money.

 Penny Pitfall

Don't get caught in flight and hungry, forced to pay big bucks for a snack. You can't get past security with a beverage, but you can pack small, unopened packages of snacks to take with you on the plane. Or pick up something after you've passed through security.

Saving While You're Away

Leaving your dollar-stretching ways at home while you travel can leave your budget aching when you return. You can apply many of the same budget-savvy tips while you're out and about at different locations. Go back to Chapters 1 through 4 and see what you can apply to your vacation travels.

The biggest way to save and still enjoy yourself is to plan your savings ahead of time. If you know you want to take advantage of an event or an experience when you're on location, call or check out their website to look for coupons and discounts before you leave.

If you'll be staying for an extended period of time or packing in a lot of activities, it might be worth it to purchase an Entertainment book for that area. You'll reap all sorts of savings, from store discounts to dining coupons to cheaper rates on a variety of activities. To purchase or to learn more, visit www.entertainment.com or call 1-888-231-SAVE (1-888-231-7283).

Getting Discounts

If time permits, make your trip less expensive and more successful by checking with the real experts—the locals. Look for message boards that discuss your destination, or visit the "community" section of Craigslist to contact locals directly. Not only will you get the inside scoop on where you're going, but you might get free money-stretching tips, too.

Be prepared to take advantage of any possible discounts for any of your affiliations. Carrying all your membership cards at all times ensures you're ready and able to cash in on any member benefits. While there are the obvious examples of AAA (American Automobile Association), AARP (American Association of Retired Persons), and Costco memberships, other, less obvious affiliations can help you cash in discounts, too. If you're a teacher, keep your school ID handy. If you or your spouse is a member of the military, carry your government-issued ID.

> **Dollar $tretcher**
>
> When you reach your destination, make a quick trip to the local Chamber of Commerce. You're sure to get free expert advice from a local who knows, as well as valuable coupons and discounts from local businesses.

If you're traveling with your school- or college-age children, be sure they also have the school ID or ASB (Associated Student Body) cards with them. Even if you're a homeschooling parent, you can purchase a homeschool ID for yourself as an educator and for your children as students. (Visit www.homeschoolID.com for more information.)

Exploring Your Dining Options

Besides the cost of transportation and lodging, your food budget will likely be your next-greatest expense while you travel. Be sure that your vacation food expenses aren't draining your wallet dry by taking advantage of any discounts your hotel may have arranged with local restaurants. Local restaurants are wise to the fact that they're vying for your business and often offer hotel guests specials to entice them. Check at the front desk before heading out for any such discounts or coupons.

Even if they can't offer you savings, they can tell you what restaurants are easy to get to, are in your budget, and—most important—have good food.

Delivery service isn't just reserved for pizza. Many restaurants in close proximity to hotels cater specifically to travelers. Not only will they deliver right to your hotel room door, but many offer special discounts and pricing as well. Next time you're hungry and don't feel like leaving the comfort of your room, call the front desk to get suggestions. You might also find such information in the hotel reference binder or welcome information left in each room. Such materials are worth a quick look because you might not only find complete delivery menus, but even coupons or "mention this ad" discounts you wouldn't have otherwise known about.

Even though cooking might be the last thing on your mind while on vacation, the amount of money you can save preparing your own food may help make it more enticing. Take advantage of hotels that offer the convenience of a small kitchenette or even just a microwave and small fridge or freezer. Even just resolving to eat breakfast or lunch in your hotel room can really stretch your budget and enable you to afford an even nicer meal out later.

Taking your dollar-stretching skills along with you on your trip—whether it be out of town or around the corner—can make any outing more rewarding. Here's to hoping only your wallet, not your baggage, bulges at the seams!

Chapter 13

Go Green to Keep More Green

In This Chapter

- ◆ Sharing car costs
- ◆ Less packaging, lower cost
- ◆ Energy- and dollar-saving tips
- ◆ DIY for more value and savings

Going green isn't just beneficial for the environment. It can also help stretch your dollar, not to mention improve your health. In fact, many resources and activities now labeled "green" have been used by devoted dollar stretchers for years.

So do your part for the earth and your wallet. Embrace a greener lifestyle to breathe cleaner air, leave less of an environmental footprint, and bank bigger savings. From driving to surfing the web, from cooking to looking beautiful, you'll see that going green saves you more green!

Becoming "Car Optional"

It should come as no surprise that public transportation can be a money saver. It can also be a hassle, especially if you're used to having your own car. Before you discount public transportation completely and move on to the next section, wait a minute. Check around your area to see if there's a rider-assistance line you can call to minimize some of the hassle and discuss all your transportation options. Doing a little homework and picking the brain of a service expert could help you get where you're going with less of a headache while saving you money.

Taking advantage of public transportation is a finance-friendly choice, but there are other options. How about paying for the convenience of a car only when you need it? Wouldn't it be great to keep more money in your pocket by sharing some of the expense of car ownership?

Share Car Ownership—and Costs

If you like the convenience of a car but don't need access to one every day, car sharing may be for you. Zipcar is a company based solely on this concept. Zipcars are parked all over cities up and down the East and West Coasts. For a nominal enrollment fee, Zipcar members receive a Zipcard that enables them to open a Zipcar after they've made a reservation either online or by phone. One wave of the Zipcard in front of the card reader in the windshield and the car door unlocks, ready for use. Vehicles, including BMWs, hybrids, even pickup trucks, can be reserved hourly (for about $9/ hour) or by the day (for about $60/ day).

> **Dollar $tretcher**
>
> Zipcards also enable members to earn various discounts throughout their community at restaurants, bookstores, and even theme parks. Zipsters can use their Zipcard to cash in on online savings as well.

Other dollar-stretching perks are included, too. Auto insurance is included, and so is your in-city parking space, gas, and mileage. Plus, you never have to worry about having to pay for car maintenance or upkeep. For more information, visit www. zipcar.com.

Get Online to Stay Out of the Car

The Internet can help you become car-optional in a variety of ways. With a computer and Internet access, you can find new ways to accomplish chores that traditionally required leaving the house.

Easiest perhaps is to shop online. From buying groceries to gifts and everything in between, if you can point and click, you can stay out of the car and still get things done. You can often find free shipping, too.

If you can, work from home. So many jobs now are reliant only on an experienced mind and a computer. If that's the case with your job and you have both, find out if your supervisor is willing to accommodate a change in job location—to your home. Working from home enables you to stretch your bucks in all kinds of ways, from money saved on eating lunch out (so you can parlay it into a dinner out!) to office clothes (which can be traded up for fancy duds!) to less gas and time spent in rush-hour commuter traffic (so you can afford a much-deserved weekend away!).

Some doctor's offices now offer e-mail consultations either with a nurse in the office or with the physician directly. If this is available to you, take advantage of it to save yourself a trip and an office visit co-pay.

Access your local public library's website to borrow books, CDs, and movies. You can either save yourself a trip by placing a hold on the item you need and then traveling only when it's available, or some libraries will mail items to you, saving you a trip out entirely. Use the money you save on a night at the movies or a fancy dessert out!

View movies online or order DVDs via mail order, and skip the trip to the theater or movie rental store completely.

Incorporating even a few of these online ideas can shave time off spent in the car, dollars spent on gasoline, and pollution spewed into the air.

Less Can Mean More

Getting more isn't always a better value. If you get more of what you need of anything, it only ends up costing you in the end. Whether it's excessive packaging that fills up your trash can and increases your waste-removal rates, or additives and chemicals in products that you really don't need, you pay and so does the environment.

Going green can help you earn money, too. Opt to bring your own reusable shopping bags with you to the grocery store, and you'll likely receive a credit per bag toward your purchase.

Less Packaging, Smaller Price

There's only one instance in which getting less actually helps you stretch your dollar, and that's packaging. Generally speaking, the less packaging an item has, the less you pay for it. Less packaging benefits the environment and saves the manufacturer money. They, in turn, pass along this savings to you.

Purchasing items in bulk is an ideal way to eliminate superfluous packaging and stretch your dollar. Many grocery stores are now catering to bulk buyers, and warehouse clubs are a popular way to volume-shop.

Buyer beware, though: shopping at warehouse clubs does not automatically guarantee you're getting the best price. You may be able to get more for less by waiting for a sale price at a traditional store or opting for a generic brand.

Get More with Multipurpose Products

Using fewer household cleaners can also keep more green in your wallet. Instead of purchasing a different product for every purpose under the sun, select products that accomplish a variety of jobs. You'll stretch your money substantially by reducing how many products you purchase, and you'll reduce the amount of valuable space they take up in your home, not to mention landfill space if you toss the empty bottles (but you would recycle them, right?).

Purchasing such products also makes it easier to buy in bulk, which can greatly increase your savings. Even if you opt not to make your own cleaners, many mass-produced green cleaners are available in bulk with directions on how to dilute for various purposes. Take advantage of the savings and the convenience, and feel good about being a responsible consumer at the same time.

Penny Pitfall _____

It's tempting to use more product to get a job done faster, but resist the urge. When removing stubborn grime, residue, stains, or unwanted adhesives, it's often not how much product you use that matters most, but rather the time you give the product to work. So let the product sit a while. You'll get the same result and use less.

Resolve to Waste Less

When you look at our society's obsession with youth and beauty, it isn't hard to believe how wasteful we've become as well. People don't get things repaired anymore. Instead, it's out with the old and out to the store to purchase a brand-new item. This way of thinking is expensive, and it's incredibly careless. All that thrown-away stuff has to go somewhere, and it's filling up landfills and endangering wildlife and our own health through contaminated water and soil. To help stop this trend, resolve to reuse and repurpose more. The environment, and your bank account, will thank you.

Dollar $tretcher _____

Stretch your dollar by shopping with repurposing in mind. By selecting an item that can serve two purposes, you get double the value. Rubber gloves are great for preventing dishpan hands, and they make great pet hair removers. Some blouses can double as lightweight jackets. Small plastic bowls are great for serving smaller portions or desserts and can double as handy prep bowls.

It makes good financial sense to repair or replace only a part rather than an entire item, but that's often easier said than done. So when purchasing an appliance, it makes good dollar-stretching sense to opt for a product from a manufacturer that's been around for a while. That way you know that if you're ever in need of a replacement part, you're much more likely to be able to find it and less likely to have to reach deep into your pocket again to completely replace the item.

What if that sounds like great advice now, but it's a little too late? Don't lose hope. If a call to the manufacturer falls flat and you're unable to find a parts store that carries what you need, try listing what you need on Craigslist. You may very well find someone willing to donate a part to your cause. If what you need isn't too brand-specific, check out a local thrift store for a similar item you can buy on the cheap to piece out for exactly what you need.

As for actually making the repair, don't be too quick to call a professional. Chances are, someone somewhere has also faced this problem and has likely posted directions on how to fix it online. Don't be afraid to give it a shot yourself. After all, it's already broken. Just take care not to do any further damage to the appliance or yourself by taking your time and using the proper tools.

New Uses for Old Items

You can also stretch your dollar by stretching your imagination. Before heading to the store to pick up a new tool for a task, see if you can find a way to use something you already own. The following list contains a few ideas to get your creative juices flowing:

♦ Use a kitchen whisk or submersion blender to create great froth and foam in milk, hot chocolate, or coffee drinks.

♦ Vegetable peelers can make quick work of shaving hard cheeses and blocks of chocolate.

♦ Slow cookers can make mulled cider and fondue a snap.

♦ Use your paper shredder (or the contents already in it) to make pretty protective packaging for gifts instead of buying tissue paper.

♦ Wrap a large rubber band on each side of a hanger to keep delicate items from falling off and ending up on the floor.

♦ Skip a garlic press and use the smallest side of your box grater to grate your garlic instead.

♦ Use yesterday's newspaper to clean and shine your windows instead of costly, smelly cleaners. (Beware of getting the ink on your hands and clothing, though!)

By using various items for more than one purpose, you'll not only save money, but you'll save your home from extra clutter and squeeze more value out of purchases you've already made.

Repurpose to Find New Value

Stretch your dollar by uncovering hidden value in things, and resolve to take a second look at items before tossing them in the trash or recycling bin. After all, every purpose we buy a product for had to first be visualized by someone else before you. Try to get in an inventor's frame of mind and see what you can reuse.

It would be impossible to list every single repurposing possibility, but the following offers a few ideas to get you started thinking like an inventor:

- Cut empty paper towel rolls along one side to create cord organizers for electronics.

- Use empty tissue boxes to dispense plastic bags.

- Use shoe and jewelry boxes as drawer organizers.

- Ice cube trays make a convenient place to store and organize jewelry and earrings.

- Use an empty soup can as a biscuit or cookie cutter.

- Plastic lids can be used as coasters or under plants to protect your tables.

- Gather mesh produce bags into a bundle and secure with a rubber band for a great cleaning scrubbie.

- Use buttons in place of lost game pieces.

> **Super Saver**
>
> Perk up your plants with your used coffee grounds. Sprinkle the grounds around the base of plants for a great, free fertilizer. The grounds slowly deliver nitrogen to the soil. They also repel ants, slugs, and snails.

The next time you think you need to head out to the store to buy something for a particular purpose, try shopping at home instead. You probably purchased many items around your house for a specific single reason, but that doesn't preclude them from serving another purpose. An open mind and a little ingenuity can help turn the tools and appliances you already have into multipurpose items.

DIY Dollar-Stretching Recipes

There's an overwhelming amount of innovative DIY solutions for different tasks, and you might be surprised that many of these valuable, money-saving lessons come from our history. By returning to doing some household tasks the way they were accomplished generations ago, you can not only stretch your dollars by spending less, but leave far less of a negative footprint on the environment as well.

For example, to keep it simple, keep it cheap, and help those with breathing difficulties, use plain baking soda around your home. Use it as a deodorizer by sprinkling it into cat litter and smelly shoes, or place a box in your fridge and freezer to absorb odors. Create a gentle abrasive cleanser by mixing it with water to clean almost anything with great results. Use it as a bath additive for softer skin, to help soothe eczema, or to relieve an insect bite or bee sting. Or use it as a nontoxic carpet deodorizer. Simply sprinkle it on, let it sit for at least 20 minutes, and vacuum to breathe easier for cheaper.

Dollar $tretcher

Effective, budget-friendly cleaning is as much about what tools you use as it is about what product. Invest in inexpensive spray bottles and a few microfiber cloths to use over and over again for great, economical results. Save even more by repurposing old T-shirts, rags, and even socks for dusting and cleaning.

Homemade Green Cleaners

Clean doesn't have a smell. It wasn't until the advent of modern chemical cleaners that we've come to associate a clean home with a scent. In fact, pets and people—especially children—can have breathing issues such as asthma or allergies thanks to these "clean" scents.

Give your checkbook and the noses in your home a break by employing green, homemade cleaners instead. They're every bit as effective and, in most cases, cost only pennies to prepare.

Dollar $tretcher

If like the idea of using nontoxic, inexpensive homemade cleaners, but miss the fresh scents, purchase a small bottle of essential oil to add to your cleaners. The initial cost of the oil may seem expensive, but it only takes a few drops to scent an entire bottle, and it lasts a very long time, making it a great value.

Green All-Purpose Cleaner

For a great nontoxic all-around spray cleaner, mix the following in a spray bottle:

½ cup white vinegar

¼ cup baking soda

½ gal. water

Use on everything from kitchen counters to shower doors to chrome fixtures. (As with any product you're using for the first time, test in an inconspicuous area first.)

Green Disinfectant

You don't have to sacrifice your dollars to get a good disinfectant. Make your own for less money by mixing the following in a spray bottle:

1 part vinegar

1 part water

Although the mixture leaves no lasting odor—the vinegar evaporates very quickly, leaving behind nothing but a clean surface—if you have a sensitive nose, use apple cider vinegar.

Green Disinfecting Wipes

Don't pay others to make your cleaning more convenient. Keep more of your money and create your own convenience cleaners. To make your own multipurpose disinfecting wipes, unwrap and accordion-fold half a roll of paper towels into any empty plastic container with a lid. Cover the paper towels with the following mixture:

½ cup vinegar

1½ cups boiled (or distilled) water

Water (enough to fill)

4 or 5 drops essential oils (optional)

If you prefer a canister-type dispenser, use a sharp knife to cut a roll of paper towels in half width-wise to create two smaller rolls. Use a pair of pliers to remove the cardboard core, and place the roll into the canister. Cover with the vinegar-water-essential-oil mixture. Pull out the wipes starting from the middle of the roll.

Dollar $tretcher

Protect your investment of money and time and store your premade mixes in airtight containers. This one-time expense will serve you well with years of dollar-stretching use.

Green Widow Cleaner

For spotless windows for pennies, combine the following in a spray bottle:

2 tsp. white vinegar

1 qt. water

Spray on windows or mirrors, and wipe clean with a repurposed rag or even newspaper. Craving that fresh lemon scent? Use ½ cup lemon juice instead of the vinegar and mix with 2 cups water.

Green Drain Cleaner

Slow drains often require expensive and highly toxic products. Spare your budget and the environment with this nontoxic home remedy instead:

½ cup baking soda

1 cup white vinegar

1 gal. hot or boiling water

Pour the baking soda into the drain, and quickly follow it with the vinegar. Let science do its magic for a few minutes, and watch the sitting mixture foam. Flush the drain clean by pouring in water last. This mixture is also great for cleaning kitchen sinks with garbage disposals.

Dollar $tretcher

Citrus peels are great for cleaning and deodorizing garbage disposals. Just toss a few peels in while the disposal is running, and your whole kitchen will smell fresh.

Green Toilet Bowl Cleaner

For a super dollar-stretching, green way to keep your toilet sparkling, mix the following in a bowl or pitcher:

¼ cup baking soda

1 cup white vinegar

Pour the mixture into your toilet bowl. The cheap combination creates a strong chemical reaction that will leave it spotless.

Green After-Shower Spray

Keep your shower clean, your dollars stretched, and your hands and knees free from scrubbing by concocting your own homemade after-shower spray. Combine the following in a spray bottle:

1 part white vinegar

2 parts water

3 tsp. tea tree oil

Keep the spray bottle in the shower, if space allows, and give the bottle a quick shake before each use. As with all after-shower sprays, be sure to give the shower a quick rinse before re-entering, to prevent slipping.

DIY Health and Beauty Savers

Want to save some money on your beauty routine and put the money into your wardrobe (or wherever else you like) instead? The following ideas help keep your medicine cabinet and your vanity stocked with green products for less:

♦ Apply used tea bags to your eyes to reduce puffiness and dark circles.

♦ Mix baking soda with water to form a paste and use as a mildly abrasive tooth whitener.

♦ Skip spending money on name-brand facial toner. Use plain witch hazel instead for the same results with fewer additives.

♦ Apply any kind of kitchen oil to your cuticles to moisturize and prevent damage. For increased effectiveness, soften your cuticles by soaking in warm water before massaging in oil.

♦ Mayonnaise, mashed avocado, and olive oil all make great conditioning treatments for dry hair.

♦ For oily hair, massage finely grated carrot through your hair and let it sit for 15 minutes. Shampoo as usual.

♦ Use a makeup brush to dab lemon juice on age spots to gently fade and lighten them.

This is by no means an exhaustive list, but these ideas show you how a little ingenuity and a creative eye can make a mountain of value out of a molehill of resources and stretch your dollar as a result. Savvy consumers and smart dollar stretchers everywhere come up with new ideas daily, so don't forget to check online for even more DIY health and beauty ideas. Because sites come and go so quickly, the best way to find these ideas is to simply do a keyword search in any search engine or join an active online community devoted to exchanging such ideas such as www.makingbysaving.com.

It's a great thing when everyone can win. When you decide to go green, that's exactly what happens. The environment is spared more damage, your needs are met, and your bank account is left with more money in it. Whether the changes you make are big or small doesn't matter because even small changes can add up.

Chapter 14

Celebrate and Still Stash Cash

In This Chapter

- ◆ Celebrate for less
- ◆ Establish new stretch-savvy traditions
- ◆ Give more, spend less
- ◆ Haul in after-holiday savings

Birthdays, graduations, weddings, and holidays are memorable times for friends and family to gather and celebrate. You want to give the people you love wonderful presents, feed them delicious meals, and make lasting memories together. But sometimes your pocketbook doesn't have your same generous spirit.

Stay steadfast in your dollar stretching and still foster lots of cheer by approaching gift-giving celebrations with creativity, a renewed appreciation for old traditions, and a willingness to create new ones.

Stretching Your Celebration Dollar

It's advertisers' job to make you think you need to spend tons of money to make your holidays bright. It's your job to recognize their tactics so you and your wallet don't suffer the consequences of spending too much.

Instead, refocus holiday activities and traditions around what really matters—family, friends, and experiences—not *things*. You'll create memories rather than creating clutter in your home, not to mention a big January credit card bill!

Celebrate the personal reasons for Christmas and other year-end holidays rather than commercially created ones. Light candles and sing songs together, and avoid spending too much time at the mall. Share stories and relive past holiday memories to keep the focus on people instead of all the holiday stuff, including gifts. Skip spending a fortune on decorations, too. Get out and enjoy how nature's decorated herself for free.

Super Saver

Place candles in the fridge for a few hours before you plan on burning them. The cooled wax will burn more slowly and give you more burning hours for your money.

Make any gift-giving opportunity appreciated and memorable without the hefty price tag by planning ahead and using some creative thinking. The vast majority of gifting occasions don't popup unscheduled; use this fact to your advantage and shop clearance racks and sales year round to find the perfect gift at a great price.

Or try taking an entirely new approach to gift giving. Why not give friends and family the gift of an experience that will create invaluable memories rather than a thing that may simply collect dust? Anyone, for example, can appreciate a wonderful homemade meal prepared just for them, and rest assured every new parent won't soon forget the thoughtful gift of a few hours of free babysitting!

Prioritize Holiday Spending

Before you completely revamp your holiday, though, it's important to be sure everyone is on the same page and onboard with making the holidays bright and your dollar go further.

At the beginning of the holiday season, decide as a household what's important. What may seem small and insignificant to you may be much more important to another family member who will be hurt if it's skipped. Sit down and make the decisions as a family, and you're more likely to be successful at creating a holiday to remember *and* at stretching your dollars without shortchanging anyone of something that really matters to them.

If you're like most families, after all the gifts are opened and the thank you's are being said, they're usually followed by "Oh, you spent too much!" Be proactive about setting a gift-giving budget before the next holiday-shopping season approaches. Get everyone involved on the discussion, and agree on a price limit. It's the thought that counts, after all, so give how much you're going to spend adequate thought also.

Having each family member only buy for one other family member is a great way to stretch your dollars, too. You can get or give one terrific present instead of the many smaller ones.

Establish New Traditions

Ongoing traditions are a big part of what make holidays so special. That doesn't mean they have to have a big price tag, though. Although we're conditioned to think that spending money on things is paramount to having a fun, meaningful holiday experience, the opposite is usually true. You can easily recapture the childlike fun of enjoying the sights and sounds of the holiday, establish new traditions, and not spend a dime. Give some thought to different, new traditions you can begin to incorporate now that will stretch your holiday dollar year after year while creating priceless memories.

For example, skip spending money on holiday spirits and get giddy on mulled cider and silly holiday songs instead. Skip the trip to an expensive show and watch your favorite holiday movies and cartoons at home. Go caroling with friends. If weather permits, go play in freshly fallen snow.

The holidays are a great time to find renewed appreciation for what we already have and refocus on the needs of others. Consider starting a new tradition to foster this each year. Save your money and your energy, and skip slaving over a huge holiday meal entirely. Instead enjoy an easier, untraditional holiday meal with friends and family, and donate the saved cash to a food bank. Save your household from added unnecessary "stuff," and make a pact with friends and family to purchase and donate to a toy drive instead.

Consider establishing new traditions for other celebrations, too. Instead of exchanging birthday gifts with friends, for example, make it a tradition to treat one another to a special something or a movie on each other's special day. You'll not only save money on not having to purchase a gift itself, not to mention the gift wrap, but you'll avoid having to rack your brain for a new idea every year and you'll always have the experience to look forward to.

Free (or Nearly Free) Holiday Ideas

You don't want to tax your wallet, but don't become a scrooge. If you've decided a particular holiday tradition is simply too expensive, replace it with a new one rather than just kill it. Making memories doesn't have to cost money; only creativity is required.

Don't spend money buying holiday decorations; make them. You'll save money, you'll have fun, and you'll help foster the importance of family and creativity over commercialism. Take a free walk to the mall to enjoy all the decorations and holiday music and get inspiration for making your own.

 Super Saver

When grocery shopping during the holidays, consider stocking up on extras you use throughout the year. Items such as butter and flour are traditionally cheaper at the holidays and store well in the freezer for later use.

Marvel at all the money you can save and fun you can have baking your own holiday treats to give as gifts.

Clay you can bake in your oven is terrific for holiday ornaments, and you can probably find a few free recipes for the dough online.

Did a winter windstorm knock down evergreen branches in your yard?

Collect and use them to decorate. You'll clean up outside and get great-smelling garland for free.

Send electronic holiday cards by e-mail rather than purchasing traditional paper ones and then paying for postage. There are many great, free websites that will help you with this service. In many cases you can even personalize it by sending pictures, too.

Local schools, churches, senior centers, and city community centers often sponsor holiday activities for families and children. You'll gain a great experience at a low cost and help your community at the same time.

Fill a holiday night with fun by driving around the neighborhood to enjoy looking at all the houses covered in twinkling lights. Foster the festive mood by playing holiday music in the car and treating everyone to hot chocolate or some other small treat.

Incorporating even just a few no-cost and low-cost holiday ideas can stretch your dollar so you'll have more to splurge on holiday treats and traditions that matter most.

 Penny Pitfall

Don't shell out big bucks for that picture with Santa. Often you can find a free Santa meet-and-greet scheduled somewhere in the community.

Stretching Your Gift-Giving Dollar

The holidays come around at the same time every year. There's no need to let them sneak up on you and your checkbook. Skip the stress of crowded streets, long lines, and hefty prices by planning well in advance. You'll be better able to relax and enjoy the season, especially knowing that maxed-out credit card bills won't be looming in January.

The retail world officially kicks off the holiday shopping season on Black Friday, but you can stretch your dollar by shopping throughout the year. You'll afford yourself time to be extra thoughtful about your purchases as well as increase your chances of getting gifts at great prices. A brief cautionary word to the wise: do take extra care in purchasing gifts too far in advance that may later need to be exchanged, however. While many stores do offer gift receipts, many of these will only honor returns or exchanges for a maximum of 30 to 90 days past the original date of purchase.

Stay organized with all your in-advance shopping by keeping a small notebook up-to-date with the information of people you purchase for. Note sizes, color preferences, and special requests so you're able to jump when a great gift opportunity presents itself. Your gift-giving notebook can also serve as a handy place to store all your store and gift receipts as well.

Dollar $tretcher

Don't let any gift-giving situations catch you—or your wallet—off guard. Avoid the lines, avoid bad traffic, and minimize your stress by designating a place in your home to stash the gifts you purchase throughout the year. Don't forget to include a few all-purpose-type gifts that would be appropriate for a wide range of recipients, too.

Black Friday Strategies

If you despise the Black Friday crowds but can't let the great prices pass you by, there is hope. Find a store that offers price adjustments, and purchase the item a day or two early. Then visit the store later to request the price adjustment. Verify in advance the store's price adjustment policies, however, as some stores won't honor price adjustments on limited-time-only specials.

Secure the dollar-stretching savings while minimizing the hassle by dividing your shopping list and conquering it with a friend. Agree ahead of time who will pick up what items at various stores. Then meet later to settle up the bill and collect your items from one another. Because time and store supplies are of the essence, you'll increase your chances of being able to snag the great sales prices at multiple stores while only visiting a one (or a few) personally.

After Black Friday comes Cyber Monday, when online retailers offer sometimes huge, one-day savings. You can find the hottest gifts of the season with deep discounts on that day. It can be worth your time to hop online and see what you can save. Shipping is often free, but even if it's not, the sales price you get might cover it and still be less expensive than what you could get in a brick-and-mortar store.

Stocking Up on Free Extras

Don't pay for gift boxes during the holiday season. With every clothing or linen purchase you make throughout the year, request a complimentary gift box. They're flat so they're easy to store, and you'll be able to accumulate a nice supply in a variety of sizes for free. Some stores also offer free tissue paper upon request as well. Empty cereal boxes also make great gift boxes. They're a great size and can be completely flattened for easy storage.

 Super Saver

Gather and save baskets, tins, and gift bags to reuse as gift packaging during the holidays as well. You can stretch your gift-wrapping dollars significantly by opting for basic wrapping paper and packaging and investing in pretty ribbons and bows to make them extra special.

Save bows from packages you receive, store them inside rolls of gift wrap, and when you need a bow to finish off a gift, bring it back to life by using a warm—not hot—curling iron to smooth out any creases in the ribbon.

If you're devoted to starting early, you can often acquire quite a collection of stocking stuffers and small gifts for absolutely free. If you're planning to make a purchase anyway, time it so you're able to take advantage of free gift opportunities and tuck away the freebies to give away later. Send away for free samples. Someone might not be thrilled to find a travel-size toothpaste in their Christmas stocking, but they might like a sample of nice lotions, facial care products, perfumes, aftershave, or a variety of cosmetics. (For a list of sites offering up-to-date free sample offers, check out Resources.)

Inexpensive Holiday Gift-Giving

There's no way around it: gift-giving is a steadfast holiday tradition. It doesn't have to be a stressful, expensive experience, though. Take control of your gift-giving ways, and show your friends and family how

Penny Pitfall

You can buy lots of gifts in advance, but hold off on gift cards. Purchase gift cards only a day or two before you plan to give them to help protect the credit balance from expiration dates and dormancy fees.

much you love them with gifts that come more from your heart than your wallet. Bake cookies, write a poem, give a photo, promise to mow someone's lawn ... there are thousands of gifts that are priceless without being pricey!

If you have children, the desire to wow them with a plentitude of pretty packages can be great. Keep your budget and your house from bursting at the seams by emphasizing quality over quantity. It's far better to spend more money on a few toys that will have longevity than spending the same amount on a bunch of toys that may not last.

Divide and conquer to create unique and inexpensive gifts of your own. Make your own chocolate assortments, gift baskets, or coffee gift packages with purchases you've made in bulk at a warehouse store. You'll be able to get excellent quality products at a great price, and you'll be able to create several gifts all at once. The time, thought, and effort that went into creating the gift will be evident, too.

If a store offers complimentary gift wrap, use it. Even if you don't want to stand in line and wait for them to do the wrapping for you, ask if you may take a small piece of wrapping paper and some ribbon with you to wrap the item later yourself. You'll not only save money on wrapping supplies, but you'll get more variety in the wrapping paper designs as well.

Super Saver

If you're shipping a gift to someone, skip the cost of foam peanuts. Use plain air-popped popcorn instead.

Gifts for Children

Consider unconventional, unique gifts for children to stretch your gift-giving dollars. The ideas are as endless as the child recipients they're meant for. The following are just a few alternative dollar-stretching gift ideas:

- A "new" wardrobe for a favorite doll comprised of baby clothes purchased at the thrift store

- An art kit made of supplies purchased during back-to-school sales

- A craft kit with glue and a hodgepodge of miscellaneous craft supplies

- A "publish-your-own-book" kit with paper and pencils for writing and editing along with a hardbound composition book and markers for "publishing"

- Cooking utensils purchased from a dollar store for a budding chef

- A dress-up kit from grown-up clothing and accessories

Less-traditional gifts for children are not only more dollar stretching, but they often give the gift of experience as well. Too many toys these days seem to do the playing for the child. It doesn't have to make noise, light up, or require batteries to ensure a child will have fun with it. Foster a child's imagination and creativity by giving gifts that require a bit more thought—and leave more in your wallet.

Gifts for Adults

Giving the gift of experience is often a good way to stretch your gift-giving dollars. Wrap up an extravagantly decorated invitation to your home for a night of homemade desserts or dinner and a movie.

Consider giving of yourself by making your own coupons to give to friends and family. If you're a talented seamstress, give a coupon offering a few hours of your services with needle and thread. If you're financial whiz, give a holiday card with your phone number inside offered as a toll-free tax help line. If baking is a breeze for you, give the ongoing gift of a pie every month.

Dollar $tretcher

Don't discredit re-gifting. If neither the recipient or the previous giver knows and the item is still in like-new condition, re-gift without guilt. What matters is that the new recipient will enjoy or be able to use the gift, not how you acquired it.

If your intended gift recipient has children, consider giving the gift of a few hours of free baby-sitting. Being able to leave children in the care of a trusted friend or family member is often the best gift anyone can receive. Your gift will be much appreciated and doesn't have to cost you a cent.

Gifts for Families

While it may seem like cheating, giving one gift to an entire family is far more economical than gifting each person. Rid yourself of any guilt and instead focus on finding the most appropriate, imaginative family gift you can. Here are some considerations:

- A "family movie night" kit with a DVD, popcorn, and some candy

- A great board game

- Family zoo membership

- A special ornament or holiday decoration to commemorate a family event

- A special edible gift the entire family can share

Any gift that fosters family togetherness and helps create priceless memories is worth its weight in gold. You just don't have to pay gold for it.

Cashing In on Clearance Racks

Anyone who's ever visited a store shortly after the holidays and glanced in the direction of the customer service desk knows the sheer multitude of gifts returned. Ever wonder what happens to those tons of items returned? They often get discounted and placed directly in the clearance bin.

For the best clearance shopping opportunities after the holidays, check stores later in the day. This gives store employees ample time to process customer returns and retag items for sale.

Returned items that simply don't sell despite a steep discount usually end up in local thrift shops. Not only do department and retail stores make great donations during this time, but so do the general public. People clearing out space at home to make room for newly gifted items or simply unloading gifts they received but don't want also make great donations during this time.

As a general rule of thumb, the best time to shop thrift stores after the holidays is earlier in the week, but later in the day, as most people make donations during the weekend and this gives employees time to sift through and price the new donations for sale.

Shopping for Next Year's Holiday

You might not be in the spirit to think about next year's holiday, but now is certainly the best time to shop for it. Before you pack away all your holiday decorations and supplies, take stock of what you'll need for next year and pick it up after the holiday for substantial savings.

If you found yourself short on lights, buy them now and pack them away, ready to use next year. If a few ornaments were casualties of this year's festivities, buy the replacements now. Consider looking for next year's holiday cards now also to have them ready to go early. You'll be gratefully better prepared next year, and you'll likely only pay pennies on the dollar.

Hitting the holiday sections of stores after the fact has other payoffs, too. You can pick up what you need now on the cheap, tuck it away for next year, and

Dollar Stretcher _____

The best time to purchase an artificial tree is right after Christmas. You'll be able to get a higher-quality tree for a fraction of the original price.

completely avoid the stress of contending with the holiday crowds next year.

Year-Round Value

Don't just think Christmas supplies at the after-the-holiday clearance racks. Stores stock their shelves with more than adequate supplies of a number of different items in the hopes to sell more of everything before the end of their fiscal year. Much of this extra stock doesn't sell and ends up deeply discounted after the beginning of January when it's time to clear shelves once more. Make this your opportunity to stretch your dollar on a number of different purchases.

Manufacturers are quick to make a holiday version of almost anything, from paper towels and tissue boxes to even cleaning supplies. Many retailers are left with a bounty of it after the special day. If you're willing to look at festive packaging around your home a bit longer, you can get these items at a deep discount.

Look for generic or solid-colored gift wrap now to use throughout the year. Red, green, gold, silver, brown, and white paper picked up now while the price is right can be personalized later with stickers and ribbon for other gift-giving situations.

 Penny Pitfall

You may be tempted to invest in new storage bins to organize all your holiday supplies before packing them away. Retailers are hoping you'll do this. Wait until mid-January or even February to buy these, and you can purchase them at a better price.

Candles are a great bargain after the holidays. Purchase them now at a tremendous savings to use throughout the year and to give as gifts. Potpourri and air fresheners are another item often sent to the clearance bin during this time. If you'd like to store it for next year, pack it tightly in a re-sealable plastic bag to preserve its strength. Be sure to store candles someplace cool so they don't melt.

For some, the holidays present the only time of year to get really dressed up. Take advantage of the great deals on party clothing and evening wear after the holidays are over. Be careful when buying ahead for children, however. You can save a ton, but the savings can be swiftly lost when the clothing is too small later. It's better to select clothing a few sizes too big or that can be easily altered. Hemlines and sleeve lengths can all be shortened, so buy a size or two ahead.

Retailers as well as department stores often expand their baking and cooking supply sections during the holidays. They plan to profit off those eager to put on the huge family feasts in November and December. If you're in the market for new cookware, baking sheets, or any other kitchen tool or gadget, check the clearance racks shortly after, and you're sure to snag a great deal.

After-the-holiday savings aren't limited to just the end of the year either. The weeks following Valentine's Day are a great time for snatching up dollar-stretching bargains. From gourmet chocolates to cozy pajamas to even luxury sheets and fancy soaps, the clearance bins are often filled to the brim with those little luxuries that demand a hefty price before the holiday. Stock up now for stretch-savvy splurging on yourself or for gifts later.

 Penny Pitfall

Don't be so fast to purchase a new calendar. Get your calendar for pennies on the dollar by waiting until after the holidays to purchase it.

The clearance racks after Valentine's Day can be filled with a great assortment of Christmas-type items as well. While it may very well be the last thing on your mind, look for red, gold, and silver wrapping paper, gift bags, bows, and ribbons you can use later on in the year.

It's not exactly clearance, but most stores hold white sales during January, when you can secure discounted prices on towels, bed linens, and comforters. Be mindful, though, that some so-called white sales aren't sales at all, but rather just overpriced home linens brought down to a reasonable price.

Retailers are banking on your New Year's resolutions to make them big profits. Many well-intentioned consumers go out and plunk down hundreds of dollars to purchase exercise and sports equipment with the hopes of improving their health and physical fitness. If you're one of them, improve the fitness of your finances, too, by stalling on your purchase. Wait until late January or February instead and pick it up at a discounted price.

Keep your holidays bright without bursting your financial bubble by maintaining your dollar-stretching ways throughout the year. After all, dollar stretching is as much about spending your money to improve your life as it is about spending less. So get out and get merry, keeping more money in your pocket to jingle all the way home.

Chapter 15

Stretching Tomorrow's Dollar Today

In This Chapter

- ◆ Extra employer benefits
- ◆ Housing considerations
- ◆ Preparing for retirement
- ◆ Tips for financing college costs

The very fact that you're reading this book makes it clear you care about your money and how much you can get for every dollar you spend. You don't want to sacrifice quality of life just becomes times are a little tougher. Often getting the best value for your future dollar means preparing and saving for tomorrow today. This chapter isn't intended to be an exhaustive list, but it is meant to illustrate ways in which stretching your dollar now can help build more value and decrease your need to pinch pennies later.

Take Advantage of Employee "Extras"

Let's face it: you likely don't work for just a paycheck. Many employers offer employees other benefits to retain a loyal workforce.

Ignorance is bliss, except when it comes to missing out on great opportunities. Be sure you're getting every possible benefit you're entitled to. It may sound obvious, but many people don't. Periodically check with your human resources representative or personnel office to find out if there are any additional employee extras or benefits you can sign up for.

Penny Pitfall

There's power in numbers, so don't forget to take advantage of it. Many employers can snag great group discounts on everything from theme park tickets to movie tickets to even zoo memberships. Don't miss out on great savings possibilities simply because you didn't ask.

If there's a benefit you'd like to see your employer offer, be sure to ask for that, too. Chances are you aren't the only one, and if you don't ask, you certainly won't receive. There's a big difference between whining and asking for benefits other employers consider standard. Benefits of any kind usually cost an employer money, so they most likely won't offer or extend them to employees unless they know a majority of their workforce wants them. Speak up, and let the company know you want them.

Life Insurance Benefits

Many employers offer life insurance for free to their employees. Even if it's only a token policy, it is potentially free money for your family should the unthinkable happen. If you're in need of a more substantial policy, inquire about signing up for a discounted group rate through the same company. There's strength in numbers, and there's definitely savings in numbers, too. Chances are good that the policy offered through your employer is also a marketing ploy by the insurance company itself to entice you to purchase a larger policy. Go ahead and do so; just be sure you're getting a discounted rate beforehand.

Employer-provided life insurance can also be a safe harbor for those with medical conditions or other situations that may preclude them from purchasing a policy on their own. In such a situation, even if you're able to secure a policy, you'll likely pay through the nose for it. This might not be case now, but even so, protect your future insurability and sign up for a token policy now. Your future bank account will appreciate the savings, and you and your family will appreciate the peace of mind.

Retirement Contribution Matching

If you're currently working for an employer that offers 401(k) matching, be sure to take advantage of it. Not doing so is paramount to throwing money out the window. Doing so, on the other hand, is like doubling your money for free later on.

Participating in a 401(k) also helps you pay less in taxes now because contributions are taken out of pretax earnings, thereby lowering the total amount of income you're actually taxed on. That's what I call a win-win-win. You win now by saving money on your taxes, you win each time you see matching contributions made by your employer, and you win tomorrow by securing your financial well-being for retirement.

Even if your employer doesn't offer a 401(k) or other retirement plan, work now to protect your future. Start a dialog with human resources or your supervisor to find out why. Even if you and your co-workers aren't unionized, you still have a voice, so make it heard. Depending on current age, you may or may not be able to count on Social Security benefits. Even if you can, it likely won't be enough to sustain your needs. Misery loves company, and if you have co-workers, you most definitely have allies in this battle. The squeaky wheel gets the oil, as they say, so start squeaking.

Smart Moves for Homeowners

Your home is likely your single largest investment. Whether it's the home of your dreams that you'll never leave or a starter home you'll resell in a few years, get the maximum value for your dollar tomorrow by making stretch-smart spending decisions today.

Build lasting value into your home regardless of your intentions to stay or sell later on. Making quality purchases when it comes to items that matter most such as appliances, windows, and flooring is just plain smart. They make your home a place you'll continue to enjoy and a home others would want to purchase as well. Know when to pay extra for the items that will have a good return on the investment and know when to skimp on items that really don't require a huge outlay of money (think cabinet pulls, faucets, and window coverings).

Protecting Resale Value

If you're not planning to own your home for the long term, protect its resale value to stretch the money you can make in the future. As much as you might want to paint an accent wall bright pink, don't. Skip the premium, plush carpet, and opt for something that's neutral and will wear well instead. Don't tear down and completely replace cabinets if simply adding new hardware will suffice. Simply put, stretch your dollars by protecting them. Don't needlessly pour money into the home that you won't get back when it's time to sell.

The easiest way to protect a home's value, however, is simply keeping everything in working order. Little problems here and there that aren't attended to quickly can add up to a major headache and an even bigger bill when it comes time to sell.

Any responsible buyer is going to pay a professional for a complete home inspection prior to purchase. Avoid leaving problems for others to find. You'll pay to fix them one way or another, either now or when it's time to settle the sale.

In It for the Long Haul

If you own your own home, it may be tempting to work harder to pay it off the closer you get to retirement. However, if the interest rate you carry on the loan is lower than the interest rate you could earn through investing the money instead, it makes more sense to do the latter.

def•i•ni•tion

A **liquid asset** is any kind of investment that can be converted to cash relatively quickly without incurring significant loss of value or associated cost.

Also worth considering is the need to maintain a good amount of *liquid assets* to help pay for rising health-care costs. Your home may very well appreciate in value, but aside from either selling or taking out a home equity loan, there's really no way to tap into the value to help pay for unanticipated costs. If you've got a good interest rate on your mortgage and a comfortable payment, leave good enough alone and invest your money elsewhere.

Knowing you already own the home you want to live in for the long haul may lure you to become complacent about your mortgage, but don't. You may very well have secured a great interest rate when you purchased the home, but don't assume rates haven't gone down since then. Call your lender and check out the competitors' rates every few years, or as the economy fluctuates, to ensure you're still locked in to a good loan program and a good rate. Should a better rate become available, educate yourself about any associated refinance fees so you can make an informed decision.

Future College Costs

I don't know a parent who doesn't want the best for his or her children. This often means a college education. If you're anything like me, the only thing worse than thinking about the total cost of a secondary education is the idea of not being able to send them at all. Your biggest defense against this hefty cost is to start early and start small. (Even if you're getting a late start, keep reading as you—and your kiddos—can still benefit!)

Regardless of what you do to begin saving for their future college costs, protect your money by making sure you're able to access and withdraw the funds for purposes other than college costs. Your child may choose a career path that doesn't require a college education, or she may be fortunate enough to earn the assistance of scholarship funds. No matter the situation, it doesn't make good money sense to invest in a way that doesn't enable you to keep full access to the money you've put away. No one knows what the future holds, but no matter where and how you invest your educational dollars, be sure you can hold on to your money in the end, regardless of the situation.

No-Loan Financing Options

If you dread the idea of taking out loans yourself or having your child begin his adult life saddled with debt, you're not alone. Fortunately, there are a number of ways to start putting small amounts of money to work today to help pay for tomorrow's college costs, no loans necessary.

A 529 plan provides an easy way to stretch out the cost of college over time by allowing someone—*anyone*—to make set deposits at predetermined intervals of time until the funds are needed for college. While student loans require the borrower to pay interest, 529 plans make your money work for you by accruing interest on the deposits.

There are two different kinds of 529 plans. One is simply a savings plan that enables you to put away money and withdraw it later, tax free, to pay for college tuition (or other eligible educational expenses). The second type enables you to lock in the price of tuition today and spread it out over time. Though the cost of tuition is locked in, most plans allow your child to choose what college or university she wants to attend.

If your state charges an income tax, you're better off taking advantage of a 529 plan specific to your state. If not, feel free to shop around, as most plans are available to all U.S. residents, and different plans do have different fee structures. No matter what plan you choose, you do not have to pay federal income tax on the interest earned.

For more information on 529 plans, including state-by-state options and withdrawal information, visit www.collegesavings.org.

Want to save for college without putting in a single dime? How about stretching the money you're already spending by making it do double-duty? Upromise is free program that enables you to earn money by buying and doing the things you already do anyway. Established in 2001, Upromise provides a way for manufacturers and companies to pay you back for using their products. For every purchase you make from an Upromise member, manufacturer, or company, you receive a deposit directly into your free Upromise account. The funds that accrue in your account can then be directly transferred to a 529 plan or simply withdrawn (even for purposes other than education). There is no charge to you.

Manufacturers and various companies pay Upromise a fee for participating in the program. Manufacturers who are members bank on the idea that you're more likely to purchase their products if they agree to give you something in return. How in the world does Upromise know when you purchase a member's product? You can register your credit cards, gas cards, or grocery store loyalty cards, or—if you don't want to register any cards—simply make purchases directly from the Upromise online mall. To learn more or to sign up, visit www.upromise.com.

Super Saver _____

If you decide to sign up for the Upromise program, get others in on the savings game, too. Ask friends and family to help you save even more by adding their information to your Upromise account. Not comfortable asking for their credit card information? No problem! Ask if you can register their grocery store loyalty cards instead.

One tried-and-true way to save for college (or retirement, for that matter) is to purchase U.S. savings bonds. The great thing about savings bonds is that you only need a small amount of money to get started, and you can purchase them whenever you have extra money in your budget. This alone makes it much more accessible to every income. On the other hand, it can take a substantial amount of time to see any real return on your investment. To learn more about the various types of savings bonds and their maturity rates, check out www.treasurydirect.gov.

Let's not forget the most obvious way to save for college—a plain old savings account. The very first step to saving for college is simply making it a priority and getting into the habit of setting the money aside to do so. Consider opening a savings account just for college costs later on. Unlike a 529 plan, you won't pay any special bookkeeping or enrollment fees. Setting up such a savings account is also much more accommodating to dollar stretching because you determine when and how much to deposit.

Dollar Stretcher _____

If friends and family are kind enough to ask for gift ideas for your child, don't hesitate to give more practical ideas such as a donation toward their college savings. Children often have a bounty of toys and their parents, a bounty of expenses. The giver can rest assured knowing their gift will be put to good use, and your budget will stretch a little further because of it.

Cut College Expenses

It makes good dollar-stretching sense to do what you can to help prevent college costs from skyrocketing to begin with. And believe it or not, there is much you can do. As with anything else in life, a little forethought and a bit of planning can make a big difference in the overall costs.

Encourage children to take advantage of Advanced Placement (AP) preparatory classes in high school. For a small fee, students can then take exams offered through the College Board and earn college credit or advanced placement. The value of the money spent on exams will be super-stretched if your child not only gains college credit, but also is able to skip prerequisite classes.

Community colleges can be a great way to start out. Not only are they far less expensive than 4-year colleges, they can also offer a more personalized education by ensuring smaller instructor-to-student ratios. (If you eventually plan to transfer the credits to a 4-year college though, contact the college or university ahead of time to ensure the credit will be accepted.)

Encourage your child to take advantage of free dual enrollment or running-start programs, too. They allow juniors and seniors in high school to enroll in college classes for both high school and college credit at the same time. Got a student already in college, or are you in college yourself? Keep the dollar stretching going and take advantage of summer classes. It's often a shorter term anyway, and graduation— and a steady paycheck—will be that much closer.

Penny Pitfall

Don't pay a premium for the convenience of purchasing your textbooks on campus. Get the exact titles of all required texts as well as their ISBN numbers and find them used, either around campus (even in the campus bookstore) or through online booksellers. Really strapped for cash? See if the text is available for checkout from a library, or split the cost and share the text with a friend.

While it's true that you don't know what tomorrow will bring, you likely know what you hope for. Don't shortchange your dreams and leave yourself pinching pennies tomorrow. Stretch today's dollar to help plan and pay for tomorrow's future. You'll enjoy peace of mind now and a deep sigh of relief later on.

Resources

The following are various resources to help you in your quest for dollar-stretching success. From great sources for coupons to travel discount sites to product pricing and review sites, you can find it here.

Cold Food Storage Chart

Sure, most everything can safely be frozen for later use, but that doesn't necessarily mean you'll want to eat it later. The following chart provides information to ensure food quality isn't sacrificed in an effort to save.

Food	In the Refrigerator (40°F or Below)	In the Freezer (0°F or Below)
Eggs (in shell)	3 to 5 weeks	don't freeze well
Egg whites		
unopened carton	10 days	up to 12 months
opened	up to 3 days	don't freeze after opened
Ground meat	1 or 2 days	3 or 4 months
Steak	3 to 5 days	6 to 12 months
Pork chops	3 to 5 days	4 to 6 months
Roast	3 to 5 days	4 to 12 months
Fresh poultry		
whole	1 or 2 days	up to 1 year
pieces	1 or 2 days	up to 9 months
Soups and stews		
vegetable or meat	3 to 4 days	2 or 3 months
Various leftovers		
Cooked meat/poultry	3 or 4 days	2 to 6 months
Chicken nuggets and patties	3 or 4 days	1 to 3 months
Pizza	3 or 4 days	1 or 2 months

Courtesy of the U.S. Department of Agriculture, Food Safety, and Inspection Service.

Coupon-Clipping Services

It's illegal to sell coupons. However, as with any service or skill, it's perfectly legal to pay someone else for their time and efforts in collecting and clipping coupons on your behalf. And believe it or not, even after paying a fee for such services, you can often come out way ahead in the form of big-time savings.

The Coupon Clippers

www.thecouponclippers.com

This full-service coupon clipping service offers very reasonable fees and fast shipping and handling times. At the time of printing, the administrative charge is 50 cents per order with a minimum order of $3 plus current postage rates.

The Coupon Master

www.thecouponmaster.com

This great coupon clipping service charges reasonable rates: administrative charge of 50 cents with a minimum $3 order plus current applicable postage rates.

eBay

www.ebay.com

Search by brand-name and the keyword *coupon*.

If you're looking for a larger quantity of coupons on specific items, eBay may well be your best bet. Here you can purchase larger lots of the same coupons in one transaction and often with a "Buy It Now" option or even a "Best Offer" opportunity, which enables you to essentially name your own price.

Coupon Sites

Think the Sunday paper is the only place to snag money-saving coupons? Think again! If you've got access to the Internet and a printer, you can search, click, print, and save. Check out the following sites to get started.

CoolSavings

www.coolsavings.com

CoolSavings is a veritable treasure trove of coupons, both printable and online, as well as price comparisons, recipes, and even an online community to connect you with others also seeking out new ways to save even more.

Coupons

www.coupons.com

If you're looking for a super fast, easy-to-maneuver site to locate and print out coupons quickly, this is it. Simply enter your zip code, and coupon savings specifically for your area will soon be yours.

Coupon Surfer
www.couponsurfer.com
This great site offers online as well as printable coupons. Again, no membership fees here either. Retailers, not you, flip for the bill.

Eversave.com
www.eversave.com
In addition to offering printable coupons, this site also offers the articles and tips to help you stretch your dollar even more.

SmartSource
www.smartsource.com
Run by News America Marketing, the same company responsible for the traditional paper coupons in Sunday papers, this site offers many of the same coupons, and you don't have to purchase a paper to get them.

Valpak
www.valpak.com
Using your zip code, search for and print valuable coupons for everything from dry cleaners to local restaurants to even local dentists.

Free Sample Sites

Nothing's better than being able to try before you buy. Check out the following sites for free samples before you plunk down your hard-earned cash for a new product.

Shop4Freebies.com
www.shop4freebies.com
This site offers one-stop-shopping convenience with the added benefit of a 5-star consumer rating system. While the site doesn't offer the free samples itself, it takes you to the source with one click.

Sweet Free Stuff
www.sweetfreestuff.com
Around since 2002, Sweetfreestuff.com is actually a blog turned free sample hub. The site is updated daily and even features an e-mail subscription option for updates.

Walmart
instoresnow.walmart.com/In-Stores-Now-Free-Samples-And-Trials.aspx
Walmart maintains a great webpage devoted to free samples for consumers. The site is updated frequently.

Major Discount Travel Sites

It is possible to see the world without spending a fortune, and the following sites can help. Do be aware that not every travel discount is offered by all the various sites, so it can really pay to check out a few before punching in your credit card information.

BookingBuddy.com
www.bookingbuddy.com
Price-check all the major travel sites as well as some lesser-known sites in one stop here.

Cheapflights.com
www.cheapflights.com
You can't book travel here, but you can preview the best deals from competing travel sites and then link to the appropriate site to complete your travel reservations.

Expedia
www.expedia.com
Go here to book discounted flights, hotel, cruises, cars, and even activities. Or you can call 1-800-EXPEDIA (1-800-397-3342) to get the same discounted rates and talk to a travel expert.

HotelRooms.com
www.hotelrooms.com
Here you can price-check hotels worldwide. The site also offers specific search options such as pet-friendly, near the airport, and budget or cheap hotels only.

Hotwire.com
www.hotwire.com
Hotwire.com books discounted flights, hotels, cruises, cars, and packages. The site also offers a "double the difference" guarantee on hotel prices. If you find a lower hotel price, it pays you double the price difference.

Orbitz
www.orbitz.com
Go here to book discounted flights, hotel, cruises, cars, activities, and rail. Orbitz also offers a price assurance guarantee: if another customer books a ticket on the same flight for a lower price, Orbitz automatically sends you the difference in cash.

Priceline.com
www.priceline.com
Priceline.com books discounted flights, hotel, cruises, cars, and packages. If you're not picky about carrier or company, you can place a bid for the amount you're willing to pay and wait for a company to accept it.

Room$aver.com
www.roomsaver.com
Search by city and state for find discounted hotel rates. Also publisher of the *Room$aver Traveler Discount Guide*, which includes valuable coupons and discounts. Find the discount guide for free at interstate-adjacent merchants nationwide or order a copy for a small fee.

Travelocity
www.travelocity.com
Travelocity books discounted flights, hotels, cruises, cars, activities, and rail. It even offers special deals on last-minute travel packages. Travelocity also has sections on its site specific to all-inclusive and gay travel deals.

Price-Comparison Sites

Don't feel like pounding the pavement to price-shop? The following sites offer great price-comparison information without all the work on your part.

BizRate
www.bizrate.com
From home and garden to hair care, BizRate.com quickly enables you to search for current price comparison information and then go to online retailers for quick, convenient purchase with just a few clicks.

Froogle
www.froogle.com
If you don't appreciate excessive advertising, you'll definitely appreciate Froogle.com. This service offered by Google gives consumers up-to-date pricing information with the added benefit of a 5-star seller rating.

NexTag
www.nextag.com
With more than 17 million visitors each month, NexTag is a price-comparison powerhouse. In addition to regular products, this site also enables consumers to search quickly for various degree programs as well as travel packages and even mortgage products.

PriceGrabber.com
www.pricegrabber.com
In addition to pricing information, PriceGrabber.com offers the added benefit of searching for products via other criteria such as free shipping and environmental impact.

PriceSCAN.com
www.pricescan.com
Another great site offering price comparisons with the added benefits of product and seller ratings, all in one convenient site.

Pricewatch
www.pricewatch.com
Around since 1995, Pricewatch offers pricing information with a less-is-more approach. Your eyes will appreciate the site's clean design and easy-to-navigate layout, and your wallet will appreciate the savings.

Online Outlet Shopping

It's no secret that outlet shopping can reap big discounts, but it might surprise you to learn that many retailers offer online outlets as well. So skip the pavement and start pounding the keyboard to seek out great outlet savings opportunities.

Dell Outlet
www.dell.com/outlet
Check out this site for refurbished computers.

eFactoryOutlets
www.efactoryoutlets.com
This is your one-stop online outlet mall for practically anything.

REI Outlet

www.rei.com/outlet

If you're looking for discounted recreational equipment, this is the site for you.

SmartBargains.com

www.smartbargains.com

Search by categories to quickly find your way to a great deal via this online outlet site.

Overstock.com

www.overstock.com

This site consistently offers not only steep discounts on products, but phenomenal shipping rates as well, stretching your dollar even more.

Product Review Sites

Why learn from your purchasing mistakes if you can avoid making them to begin with? Learn from the purchases and experiences of others by visiting any of the following sites before shelling out any of your money.

Buzzillions.com

www.buzzillions.com

This site collects product reviews from major companies such as Staples, Toys 'R' Us, and Zappos and displays them all in one convenient site.

Consumer Reports

www.consumerreports.org

Consumer Reports offers unbiased expert reviews and ratings on numerous products and services.

Epinions.com

www.epinions.com

In addition to offering access to thousands of product reviews, Epinions.com also features consumer reviews of services and even an active online community for its members.

Index